DAN-26 DANTES SUBJECT STANDARDIZED TESTS (DSST)

This is your PASSBOOK for...

Introduction to Management

Test Preparation Study Guide
Questions & Answers

NLC®
NATIONAL LEARNING CORPORATION®

National Learning Corporation

212 Michael Drive, Syosset, NY 11791
(516) 921-8888 • www.passbooks.com
E-mail: info@passbooks.com

PUBLISHED IN THE UNITED STATES OF AMERICA

PASSBOOK® SERIES

THE *PASSBOOK® SERIES* has been created to prepare applicants and candidates for the ultimate academic battlefield – the examination room.

At some time in our lives, each and every one of us may be required to take an examination – for validation, matriculation, admission, qualification, registration, certification, or licensure.

Based on the assumption that every applicant or candidate has met the basic formal educational standards, has taken the required number of courses, and read the necessary texts, the *PASSBOOK® SERIES* furnishes the one special preparation which may assure passing with confidence, instead of failing with insecurity. Examination questions – together with answers – are furnished as the basic vehicle for study so that the mysteries of the examination and its compounding difficulties may be eliminated or diminished by a sure method.

This book is meant to help you pass your examination provided that you qualify and are serious in your objective.

The entire field is reviewed through the huge store of content information which is succinctly presented through a provocative and challenging approach – the question-and-answer method.

A climate of success is established by furnishing the correct answers at the end of each test.

You soon learn to recognize types of questions, forms of questions, and patterns of questioning. You may even begin to anticipate expected outcomes.

You perceive that many questions are repeated or adapted so that you can gain acute insights, which may enable you to score many sure points.

You learn how to confront new questions, or types of questions, and to attack them confidently and work out the correct answers.

You note objectives and emphases, and recognize pitfalls and dangers, so that you may make positive educational adjustments.

Moreover, you are kept fully informed in relation to new concepts, methods, practices, and directions in the field.

You discover that you are actually taking the examination all the time: you are preparing for the examination by "taking" an examination, not by reading extraneous and/or supererogatory textbooks.

In short, this PASSBOOK®, used directedly, should be an important factor in helping you to pass your test.

NONTRADITIONAL EDUCATION

Students returning to school as adults bring more varied experience to their studies than do the teenagers who begin college shortly after graduating from high school. As a result, there are numerous programs for students with nontraditional learning curves. Hundreds of colleges and universities grant degrees to people who cannot attend classes at a regular campus or have already learned what the college is supposed to teach.

You can earn nontraditional education credits in many ways:

- Passing standardized exams
- Demonstrating knowledge gained through experience
- Completing campus-based coursework, and
- Taking courses off campus

Some methods of assessing learning for credit are objective, such as standardized tests. Others are more subjective, such as a review of life experiences.

With some help from four hypothetical characters – Alice, Vin, Lynette, and Jorge – this article describes nontraditional ways of earning educational credit. It begins by describing programs in which you can earn a high school diploma without spending 4 years in a classroom. The college picture is more complicated, so it is presented in two parts: one on gaining credit for what you know through course work or experience, and a second on college degree programs. The final section lists resources for locating more information.

Earning High School Credit

People who were prevented from finishing high school as teenagers have several options if they want to do so as adults. Some major cities have back-to-school programs that allow adults to attend high school classes with current students. But the more practical alternatives for most adults are to take the General Educational Development (GED) tests or to earn a high school diploma by demonstrating their skills or taking correspondence classes.

Of course, these options do not match the experience of staying in high school and graduating with one's friends. But they are viable alternatives for adult learners committed to meeting and, often, continuing their educational goals.

GED Program

Alice quit high school her sophomore year and took a job to help support herself, her younger brother, and their newly widowed mother. Now an adult, she wants to earn her high school diploma – and then go on to college. Because her job as head cook and her family responsibilities keep her busy during the day, she plans to get a high school equivalency diploma. She will study for, and take, the GED tests. Every year, about half a million adults earn their high school credentials this way. A GED diploma is accepted in lieu of a high school one by more than 90 percent of employers, colleges, and universities, so it is a good choice for someone like Alice.

The GED testing program is sponsored by the American Council on Education and State and local education departments. It consists of examinations in five subject areas: Writing, science, mathematics, social studies, and literature and the arts. The tests also measure skills such as analytical ability, problem solving, reading comprehension, and ability to understand and apply information. Most of the questions are multiple choice; the writing test includes an essay section on a topic of general interest.

Eligibility rules for taking the exams vary, but some states require that you must be at least 18. Tests are given in English, Spanish, and French. In addition to standard print, versions in large print, Braille, and audiocassette are also available. Total time allotted for the tests is 7 1/2 hours.

The GED tests are not easy. About one-fourth of those who complete the exams every year do not pass. Passing scores are established by administering the tests to a sample of graduating high school seniors. The minimum standard score is set so that about one-third of graduating seniors would not pass the tests if they took them.

Because of the difficulty of the tests, people need to prepare themselves to take them. Often, they start by taking the Official GED Practice Tests, usually available through a local adult education center. Centers are listed in your phone book's blue pages under "Adult Education," "Continuing Education," or "GED." Adult education centers also have information about GED preparation classes and self-study materials. Classes are generally arranged to accommodate adults' work schedules. National Learning Corporation publishes several study guides that aim to thoroughly prepare test-takers for the GED.

School districts, colleges, adult education centers, and community organizations have information about GED testing schedules and practice tests. For more information, contact them, your nearest GED testing center, or:

GED Testing Service
One Dupont Circle, NW, Suite 250
Washington, DC 20036-1163
1(800) 62-MY GED (626-9433)
(202) 939-9490

Skills Demonstration

Adults who have acquired high school level skills through experience might be eligible for the National External Diploma Program. This alternative to the GED does not involve any direct instruction. Instead, adults seeking a high school diploma must demonstrate mastery of 65 competencies in 8 general areas: Communication; computation; occupational preparedness; and self, social, consumer, scientific, and technological awareness.

Mastery is shown through the completion of the tasks. For example, a participant could prove competency in computation by measuring a room for carpeting, figuring out the amount of carpet needed, and computing the cost.

Before being accepted for the program, adults undergo an evaluation. Tests taken at one of the program's offices measure reading, writing, and mathematics abilities. A take-home segment includes a self-assessment of current skills, an individual skill evaluation, and an occupational interest and aptitude test.

Adults accepted for the program have weekly meetings with an assessor. At the meeting, the assessor reviews the participant's work from the previous week. If the task has not been completed properly, the assessor explains the mistake. Participants continue to correct their errors until they master each competency. A high school diploma is awarded upon proven mastery of all 65 competencies.

Fourteen States and the District of Columbia now offer the External Diploma Program. For more information, contact:

External Diploma Program
One Dupont Circle, NW, Suite 250
Washington, DC 20036-1193
(202) 939-9475

Correspondence and Distance Study

Vin dropped out of high school during his junior year because his family's frequent moves made it difficult for him to continue his studies. He promised himself at the time he dropped out that he would someday finish the courses needed for his diploma. For people like Vin, who prefer to earn a traditional diploma in a nontraditional way, there are about a dozen accredited courses of study for earning a high school diploma by correspondence, or distance study. The programs are either privately run, affiliated with a university, or administered by a State education department.

Distance study diploma programs have no residency requirements, allowing students to continue their studies from almost any location. Depending on the course of study, students need not be enrolled full time and usually have more flexible schedules for finishing their work. Selection of courses ranges from vo-tech to college prep, and some programs place different emphasis on the types of diplomas offered. University affiliated schools, for example, allow qualified students to take college courses along with their high school ones. Students can then apply the college credits toward a degree at that university or transfer them to another institution.

Taking courses by distance study is often more challenging and time consuming than attending classes, especially for adults who have other obligations. Success depends on each student's motivation. Students usually do reading assignments on their own. Written exercises, which they complete and send to an instructor for grading, supplement their reading material.

A list of some accredited high schools that offer diplomas by distance study is available free from the Distance Education and Training Council, formerly known as the National Home Study Council. Request the "DETC Directory of Accredited Institutions" from:

The Distance Education and Training Council
1601 18th Street, NW.
Washington, DC 20009-2529
(202) 234-5100

Some publications profiling nontraditional college programs include addresses and descriptions of several high school correspondence ones. See the Resources section at the end of this article for more information.

Getting College Credit For What You Know

Adults can receive college credit for prior coursework, by passing examinations, and documenting experiential learning. With help from a college advisor, nontraditional students should assess their skills, establish their educational goals, and determine the number of college credits they might be eligible for.

Even before you meet with a college advisor, you should collect all your school and training records. Then, make a list of all knowledge and abilities acquired through experience, no matter how irrelevant they seem to your chosen field. Next, determine your educational goals: What specific field do you wish to study? What kind of a degree do you want? Finally, determine how your past work fits into the field of study. Later on, you will evaluate educational programs to find one that's right for you.

People who have complex educational or experiential learning histories might want to have their learning evaluated by the Regents Credit Bank. The Credit Bank, operated by Regents College of the University of the State of New York, allows people to consolidate credits earned through college, experience, or other methods. Special assessments are available for Regents College enrollees whose knowledge in a specific field cannot be adequately evaluated by standardized exams. For more information, contact the Regents Credit Bank at:

Regents College
7 Columbia Circle
Albany, NY 12203-5159
(518) 464-8500

Credit For Prior College Coursework

When Lynette was in college during the 1970s, she attended several different schools and took a variety of courses. She did well in some classes and poorly in others. Now that she is a successful business owner and has more focus, Lynette thinks she should forget about her previous coursework and start from scratch. Instead, she should start from where she is.

Lynette should have all her transcripts sent to the colleges or universities of her choice and let an admissions officer determine which classes are applicable toward a degree. A few credits here and there may not seem like much, but they add up. Even if the subjects do not seem relevant to any major, they might be counted as elective credits toward a degree. And comparing the cost of transcripts with the cost of college courses, it makes sense to spend a few dollars per transcript for a chance to save hundreds, and perhaps thousands, of dollars in books and tuition.

Rules for transferring credits apply to all prior coursework at accredited colleges and universities, whether done on campus or off. Courses completed off campus, often called extended learning, include those available to students through independent study and correspondence. Many schools have extended learning programs; Brigham Young University, for example, offers more than 300 courses through its Department of Independent Study. One type of extended learning is distance learning, a form of correspondence study by technological means such as television, video and audio, CD-ROM, electronic mail, and computer tutorials. See the Resources section at the end of this article for more information about publications available from the National University Continuing Education Association.

Any previously earned college credits should be considered for transfer, no matter what the subject or the grade received. Many schools do not accept the transfer of courses graded below a C or ones taken more than a designated number of years ago. Some colleges and universities also have limits on the number of credits that can be transferred and applied toward a degree. But not all do. For example, Thomas Edison State College, New Jersey's State college for adults, accepts the transfer of all 120 hours of credit required for a baccalaureate degree – provided all the credits are transferred from regionally accredited schools, no more than 80 are at the junior college level, and the student's grades overall and in the field of study average out to C.

To assign credit for prior coursework, most schools require original transcripts. This means you must complete a form or send a written, signed request to have your transcripts released directly to a college or university. Once you have chosen the schools you want to apply to, contact the schools you attended before. Find out how much each transcript costs, and ask them to send your transcripts to the ones you are applying to. Write a letter that includes your name (and names used during attendance, if different) and dates of attendance, along with the names and addresses of the schools to which your transcripts should be sent. Include payment and mail to the registrar at the schools you have attended. The registrar's office will process your request and send an official transcript of your coursework to the colleges or universities you have designated.

Credit For Noncollege Courses

Colleges and universities are not the only ones that offer classes. Volunteer organizations and employers often provide formal training worth college credit. The American Council on Education has two programs that assess thousands of specific courses and make recommendations on the amount of college credit they are worth. Colleges and universities accept the recommendations or use them as guidelines.

One program evaluates educational courses sponsored by government agencies, business and industry, labor unions, and professional and voluntary organizations. It is the Program on Noncollegiate Sponsored Instruction (PONSI). Some of the training seminars Alice has participated in covered topics such as food preparation, kitchen safety, and nutrition. Although she has not yet earned her GED, Alice can earn college credit because of her completion of these formal job-training seminars. The number of credits each seminar is worth does not hinge on Alice's current eligibility for college enrollment.

The other program evaluates courses offered by the Army, Navy, Air Force, Marines, Coast Guard, and Department of Defense. It is the Military Evaluations Program. Jorge has never attended college, but the engineering technology classes he completed as part of his military training are worth college credit. And as an Army veteran, Jorge is eligible for a service that takes the evaluations one step further. The Army/American Council on Education Registry Transcript System (AARTS) will provide Jorge with an individualized transcript of American Council on Education credit recommendations for all courses he completed, the military occupational specialties (MOS's) he held, and examinations he passed while in the Army. All Army and National Guard enlisted personnel and veterans who enlisted after October 1981 are eligible for the transcript. Similar services are being considered by the Navy and Marine Corps.

To obtain a free transcript, see your Army Education Center for a 5454R transcript request form. Include your name, Social Security number, basic active service date, and complete address where you want the transcript sent. Mail your request to:

AARTS Operations Center
415 McPherson Ave.
Fort Leavenworth, KS 66027-1373

Recommendations for PONSI are published in *The National Guide to Educational Credit for Training Programs;* military program recommendations are in *The Guide to the Evaluation of Educational Experiences in the Armed Forces.* See the Resources section at the end of this article for more information about these publications.

Former military personnel who took a foreign language course through the Defense Language Institute may request course transcripts by sending their name, Social Security number, course title, duration of the course, and graduation date to:

Commandant, Defense Language Institute
Attn: ATFL-DAA-AR
Transcripts
Presidio of Monterey
Monterey, CA 93944-5006

Not all of Jorge's and Alice's courses have been assessed by the American Council on Education. Training courses that have no Council credit recommendation should still be assessed by an advisor at the schools they want to attend. Course descriptions, class notes, test scores, and other documentation may be helpful for comparing training courses to their college equivalents. An oral examination or other demonstration of competency might also be required.

There is no guarantee you will receive all the credits you are seeking – but you certainly won't if you make no attempt.

Credit By Examination

Standardized tests are the best-known method of receiving college credit without taking courses. These exams are often taken by high school students seeking advanced placement for college, but they are also available to adult learners. Testing programs and colleges and universities offer exams in a number of subjects. Two U.S. Government institutes have foreign language exams for employees that also may be worth college credit.

It is important to understand that receiving a passing score on these exams does not mean you get college credit automatically. Each school determines which test results it will accept, minimum scores required, how scores are converted for credit, and the amount of credit, if any, to be assigned. Most colleges and universities accept the American Council on Education credit recommendations, published every other year in the 250-page *Guide to Educational Credit by Examination.* For more information, contact:

The American Council on Education
Credit by Examination Program
One Dupont Circle, Suite 250
Washington, DC 20036-1193
(202) 939-9434

Testing programs:

You might know some of the five national testing programs by their acronyms or initials: CLEP, ACT PEP: RCE, DANTES, AP, and NOCTI. (The meanings of these initialisms are explained below.) There is some overlap among programs; for example, four of them have introductory accounting exams. Since you will not be awarded credit more than once for a specific subject, you should carefully evaluate each program for the subject exams you wish to take. And before taking an exam, make sure you will be awarded credit by the college or university you plan to attend.

CLEP (College-Level Examination Program), administered by the College Board, is the most widely accepted of the national testing programs; more than 2,800 accredited schools award credit for passing exam scores. Each test covers material taught in basic undergraduate courses. There are five general exams – English composition, humanities, college mathematics, natural sciences, and social sciences and history – and many subject exams. Most exams are entirely multiple-choice, but English composition exams may include an essay section. For more information, contact:

CLEP
P.O. Box 6600
Princeton, NJ 08541-6600
(609) 771-7865

ACT PEP: RCE (American College Testing Proficiency Exam Program: Regents College Examinations) tests are given in 38 subjects within arts and sciences, business, education, and nursing. Each exam is recommended for either lower- or upper-level credit. Exams contain either objective or extended response questions, and are graded according to a standard score, letter grade, or pass/fail. Fees vary, depending on the subject and type of exam. For more information or to request free study guides, contact:

ACT PEP: Regents College Examinations
P.O. Box 4014
Iowa City, IA 52243
(319) 337-1387
(New York State residents must contact Regents College directly.)

DANTES (Defense Activity for Nontraditional Education Support) standardized tests are developed by the Educational Testing Service for the Department of Defense. Originally administered only to military personnel, the exams have been available to the public since 1983. About 50 subject tests cover business, mathematics, social science, physical science, humanities, foreign languages, and applied technology. Most of the tests consist entirely of multiple-choice questions. Schools determine their own administering fees and testing schedules. For more information or to request free study sheets, contact:

DANTES Program Office
Mail Stop 31-X
Educational Testing Service
Princeton, NJ 08541
1(800) 257-9484

The AP (Advanced Placement) Program is a cooperative effort between secondary schools and colleges and universities. AP exams are developed each year by committees of college and high school faculty appointed by the College Board and assisted by consultants from the Educational Testing Service. Subjects include arts and languages, natural sciences, computer science, social sciences, history, and mathematics. Most tests are 2 or 3 hours long and include both multiple-choice and essay questions. AP courses are available to help students prepare for exams, which are offered in the spring. For more information about the Advanced Placement Program, contact:

Advanced Placement Services
P.O. Box 6671
Princeton, NJ 08541-6671
(609) 771-7300

NOCTI (National Occupational Competency Testing Institute) assessments are designed for people like Alice, who have vocational-technical skills that cannot be evaluated by other tests. NOCTI assesses competency at two levels: Student/job ready and teacher/experienced worker. Standardized evaluations are available for occupations such as auto-body repair, electronics, mechanical drafting, quantity food preparation, and upholstering. The tests consist of multiple-choice questions and a performance component. Other services include workshops, customized assessments, and pre-testing. For more information, contact:

NOCTI
500 N. Bronson Ave.
Ferris State University
Big Rapids, MI 49307
(616) 796-4699

Colleges and universities:

Many colleges and universities have credit-by-exam programs, through which students earn credit by passing a comprehensive exam for a course offered by the institution. Among the most widely recognized are the programs at Ohio University, the University of North Carolina, Thomas Edison State College, and New York University.

Ohio University offers about 150 examinations for credit. In addition, you may sometimes arrange to take special examinations in non-laboratory courses offered at Ohio University. To take a test for credit, you must enroll in the course. If you plan to transfer the credit earned, you also need written permission from an official at your school. Books and study materials are available, for a cost, through the university. Exams must be taken within 6 months of the enrollment date; most last 3 hours. You may arrange to take the exam off campus if you do not live near the university.

Ohio University is on the quarter-hour system; most courses are worth 4 quarter hours, the equivalent of 3 semester hours. For more information, contact:

Independent Study
Tupper Hall 302
Ohio University
Athens, OH 45701-2979
1(800) 444-2910
(614) 593-2910

The University of North Carolina offers a credit-by-examination option for 140 independent study (correspondence) courses in foreign languages, humanities, social sciences, mathematics, business administration, education, electrical and computer engineering, health administration, and natural sciences. To take an exam, you must request and receive approval from both the course instructor and the independent studies department. Exams must be taken within six months of enrollment, and you may register for no more than two at a time. If you are not near the University's Chapel Hill campus, you may take your exam under supervision at an accredited college, university, community college, or technical institute. For more information, contact:

Independent Studies
CB #1020, The Friday Center
UNC-Chapel Hill
Chapel Hill, NC 27599-1020
1(800) 862-5669 / (919) 962-1134

The Thomas Edison College Examination Program offers more than 50 exams in liberal arts, business, and professional areas. Thomas Edison State College administers tests twice a month in Trenton, New Jersey; however, students may arrange to take their tests with a proctor at any accredited American college or university or U.S. military base. Most of the tests are multiple choice; some also include short answer or essay questions. Time limits range from 90 minutes to 4 hours, depending on the exam. For more information, contact:

Thomas Edison State College
TECEP, Office of Testing and Assessment
101 W. State Street
Trenton, NJ 08608-1176
(609) 633-2844

New York University's Foreign Language Program offers proficiency exams in more than 40 languages, from Albanian to Yiddish. Two exams are available in each language: The 12-point test is equivalent to 4 undergraduate semesters, and the 16-point exam may lead to upper level credit. The tests are given at the university's Foreign Language Department throughout the year.

Proof of foreign language proficiency does not guarantee college credit. Some colleges and universities accept transcripts only for languages commonly taught, such as French and Spanish. Nontraditional programs are more likely than traditional ones to grant credit for proficiency in other languages.

For an informational brochure and registration form for NYU's foreign language proficiency exams, contact:

New York University
Foreign Language Department
48 Cooper Square, Room 107
New York, NY 10003
(212) 998-7030

Government institutes:

The Defense Language Institute and Foreign Service Institute administer foreign language proficiency exams for personnel stationed abroad. Usually, the tests are given at the end of intensive language courses or upon completion of service overseas. But some people – like Jorge, who knows Spanish – speak another language fluently and may be allowed to take a proficiency exam in that language before completing their tour of duty. Contact one of the offices listed below to obtain transcripts of those scores. Proof of proficiency does not guarantee college credit, however, as discussed above.

To request score reports from the Defense Language Institute for Defense Language Proficiency Tests, send your name, Social Security number, language for which you were tested, and, most importantly, when and where you took the exam to:

Commandant, Defense Language Institute
Attn: ATFL-ES-T
DLPT Score Report Request
Presidio of Monterey
Monterey, CA 93944-5006

To request transcripts of scores for Foreign Service Institute exams, send your name, Social Security number, language for which you were tested, and dates or year of exams to:

Foreign Service Institute
Arlington Hall
4020 Arlington Boulevard
Rosslyn, VA 22204-1500
Attn: Testing Office (Send your request to the attention of the testing office of the foreign language in which you were tested)

Credit For Experience

Experiential learning credit may be given for knowledge gained through job responsibilities, personal hobbies, volunteer opportunities, homemaking, and other experiences. Colleges and universities base credit awards on the knowledge you have attained, not for the experience alone. In addition, the knowledge must be college level; not just any learning will do. Throwing horseshoes as a hobby is not likely to be worth college credit. But if you've done research on how and where the sport originated, visited blacksmiths, organized tournaments, and written a column for a trade journal – well, that's a horseshoe of a different color.

Adults attempting to get credit for their experience should be forewarned: Having your experience evaluated for college credit is time-consuming, tedious work – not an easy shortcut for people who want quick-fix college credits. And not all experience, no matter how valuable, is the equivalent of college courses.

Requesting college credit for your experiential learning can be tricky. You should get assistance from a credit evaluations officer at the school you plan to attend, but you should also have a general idea of what your knowledge is worth. A common method for converting knowledge into credit is to use a college catalog. Find course titles and descriptions that match what you have learned through experience, and request the number of credits offered for those courses.

Once you know what credit to ask for, you must usually present your case in writing to officials at the college you plan to attend. The most common form of presenting experiential learning for credit is the portfolio. A portfolio is a written record of your knowledge along with a request for equivalent college credit. It includes an identification and description of the knowledge for which you are requesting credit, an explanatory essay of how the knowledge was gained and how it fits into your educational plans, documentation that you have acquired such knowledge, and a request for college credit. Required elements of a portfolio vary by schools but generally follow those guidelines.

In identifying knowledge you have gained, be specific about exactly what you have learned. For example, it is not enough for Lynette to say she runs a business. She must identify the knowledge she has gained from running it, such as personnel management, tax law, marketing strategy, and inventory review. She must also include brief descriptions about her knowledge of each to support her claims of having those skills.

The essay gives you a chance to relay something about who you are. It should address your educational goals, include relevant autobiographical details, and be well organized, neat, and convey confidence. In his essay, Jorge might first state his goal of becoming an engineer. Then he would explain why he joined the Army, where he got hands-on training and experience in developing and servicing electronic equipment.

This, he would say, led to his hobby of creating remote-controlled model cars, of which he has built 20. His conclusion would highlight his accomplishments and tie them to his desire to become an electronic engineer.

Documentation is evidence that you've learned what you claim to have learned. You can show proof of knowledge in a variety of ways, including audio or video recordings, letters from current or former employers describing your specific duties and job performance, blueprints, photographs or artwork, and transcripts of certifying exams for professional licenses and certification – such as Alice's certification from the American Culinary Federation. Although documentation can take many forms, written proof alone is not always enough. If it is impossible to document your knowledge in writing, find out if your experiential learning can be assessed through supplemental oral exams by a faculty expert.

Earning a College Degree

Nontraditional students often have work, family, and financial obligations that prevent them from quitting their jobs to attend school full time. Can they still meet their educational goals? Yes.

More than 150 accredited colleges and universities have nontraditional bachelor's degree programs that require students to spend little or no time on campus; over 300 others have nontraditional campus-based degree programs. Some of those schools, as well as most junior and community colleges, offer associate's degrees nontraditionally. Each school with a nontraditional course of study determines its own rules for awarding credit for prior coursework, exams, or experience, as discussed previously. Most have charges on top of tuition for providing these special services.

Several publications profile nontraditional degree programs; see the Resources section at the end of this article for more information. To determine which school best fits your academic profile and educational goals, first list your criteria. Then, evaluate nontraditional programs based on their accreditation, features, residency requirements, and expenses. Once you have chosen several schools to explore further, write to them for more information. Detailed explanations of school policies should help you decide which ones you want to apply to.

Get beyond the printed word – especially the glowing words each school writes about itself. Check out the schools you are considering with higher education authorities, alumni, employers, family members, and friends. If possible, visit the campus to talk to students and instructors and sit in on a few classes, even if you will be completing most or all of your work off campus. Ask school officials questions about such things as enrollment numbers, graduation rate, faculty qualifications, and confusing details about the application process or academic policies. After you have thoroughly investigated each prospective college or university, you can make an informed decision about which is right for you.

Accreditation

Accreditation is a process colleges and universities submit to voluntarily for getting their credentials. An accredited school has been investigated and visited by teams of observers and has periodic inspections by a private accrediting agency. The initial review can take two years or more.

Regional agencies accredit entire schools, and professional agencies accredit either specialized schools or departments within schools. Although there are no national accrediting standards, not just any accreditation will do. Countless "accreditation associations" have been invented by schools, many of which have no academic programs and sell phony degrees, to accredit themselves. But 6 regional and about 80 professional accrediting associations in the United States are recognized by the U.S. Department of Education or the Commission on Recognition of Postsecondary Accreditation. When checking accreditation, these are the names to look for. For more information about accreditation and accrediting agencies, contact:

Institutional Participation Oversight Service Accreditation and State Liaison Division
U.S. Department of Education
ROB 3, Room 3915
600 Independence Ave., SW
Washington, DC 20202-5244
(202) 708-7417

Because accreditation is not mandatory, lack of accreditation does not necessarily mean a school or program is bad. Some schools choose not to apply for accreditation, are in the process of applying, or have educational methods too unconventional for an accrediting association's standards. For the nontraditional student, however, earning a degree from a college or university with recognized accreditation is an especially important consideration. Although nontraditional education is becoming more widely accepted, it is not yet mainstream. Employers skeptical of a degree earned in a nontraditional manner are likely to be even less accepting of one from an unaccredited school.

Program Features

Because nontraditional students have diverse educational objectives, nontraditional schools are diverse in what they offer. Some programs are geared toward helping students organize their scattered educational credits to get a degree as quickly as possible. Others cater to those who may have specific credits or experience but need assistance in completing requirements. Whatever your educational profile, you should look for a program that works with you in obtaining your educational goals.

A few nontraditional programs have special admissions policies for adult learners like Alice, who plan to earn their GEDs but want to enroll in college in the meantime. Other features of nontraditional programs include individualized learning agreements, intensive academic counseling, cooperative learning and internship placement, and waiver of some prerequisites or other requirements – as well as college credit for prior coursework, examinations, and experiential learning, all discussed previously.

Lynette, whose primary goal is to finish her degree, wants to earn maximum credits for her business experience. She will look for programs that do not limit the number of credits awarded for equivalency exams and experiential learning. And since well-documented proof of knowledge is essential for earning experiential learning credits, Lynette should make sure the program she chooses provides assistance to students submitting a portfolio.

Jorge, on the other hand, has more credits than he needs in certain areas and is willing to forego some. To become an engineer, he must have a bachelor's degree; but because he is accustomed to hands-on learning, Jorge is interested in getting experience as he gains more technical skills. He will concentrate on finding schools with strong cooperative education, supervised fieldwork, or internship programs.

Residency Requirements

Programs are sometimes deemed nontraditional because of their residency requirements. Many people think of residency for colleges and universities in terms of tuition, with in-state students paying less than out-of-state ones. Residency also may refer to where a student lives, either on or off campus, while attending school.

But in nontraditional education, residency usually refers to how much time students must spend on campus, regardless of whether they attend classes there. In some nontraditional programs, students need not ever step foot on campus. Others require only a very short residency, such as one day or a few weeks. Many schools have standard residency requirements of several semesters but schedule classes for evenings or weekends to accommodate working adults.

Lynette, who previously took courses by independent study, prefers to earn credits by distance study. She will focus on schools that have no residency requirement. Several colleges and universities have nonresident degree completion programs for adults with some college credit. Under the direction of a faculty advisor, students devise a plan for earning their remaining credits. Methods for earning credits include independent study, distance learning, seminars, supervised fieldwork, and group study at arranged sites. Students may have to earn a certain number of credits through the degree-granting institution. But many programs allow students to take courses at accredited schools of their choice for transfer toward their degree.

Alice wants to attend lectures but has an unpredictable schedule. Her best course of action will be to seek out short residency programs that require students to attend seminars once or twice a semester. She can take courses that are televised and videotape them to watch when her schedule permits, with the seminars helping to ensure that she properly completes her coursework. Many colleges and universities with short residency requirements also permit students to earn some credits elsewhere, by whatever means the student chooses.

Some fields of study require classroom instruction. As Jorge will discover, few colleges and universities allow students to earn a bachelor's degree in engineering entirely through independent study. Nontraditional residency programs are designed to accommodate adults' daytime work schedules. Jorge should look for programs offering evening, weekend, summer, and accelerated courses.

Tuition and Other Expenses

The final decisions about which schools Alice, Jorge, and Lynette attend may hinge in large part on a single issue: Cost. And rising tuition is only part of the equation. Beginning with application fees and continuing through graduation fees, college expenses add up.

Traditional and nontraditional students have some expenses in common, such as the cost of books and other materials. Tuition might even be the same for some courses, especially for colleges and universities offering standard ones at unusual times. But for nontraditional programs, students may also pay fees for services such as credit or transcript review, evaluation, advisement, and portfolio assessment.

Students are also responsible for postage and handling or setup expenses for independent study courses, as well as for all examination and transcript fees for transferring credits. Usually, the more nontraditional the program, the more detailed the fees. Some schools charge a yearly enrollment fee rather than tuition for degree completion candidates who want their files to remain active.

Although tuition and fees might seem expensive, most educators tell you not to let money come between you and your educational goals. Talk to someone in the financial aid department of the school you plan to attend or check your library for publications about financial aid sources. The U.S. Department of Education publishes a guide to Federal aid programs such as Pell Grants, student loans, and work-study. To order the free 74-page booklet, *The Student Guide: Financial Aid from the U.S. Department of Education,* contact:

Federal Student Aid Information Center
P.O. Box 84
Washington, DC 20044
1 (800) 4FED-AID (433-3243)

Resources

Information on how to earn a high school diploma or college degree without following the usual routes is available from several organizations and in numerous publications. Information on nontraditional graduate degree programs, available for master's through doctoral level, though not discussed in this article, can usually be obtained from the same resources that detail bachelor's degree programs.

National Learning Corporation publishes study guides for all of these exams, for both general examinations and tests in specific subject areas. To order study guides, or to browse their catalog featuring more than 5,000 titles, visit NLC online at www.passbooks.com, or contact them by phone at (800) 632-8888.

Organizations

Adult learners should always contact their local school system, community college, or university to learn about programs that are readily available. The following national organizations can also supply information:

American Council on Education
One Dupont Circle
Washington, DC 20036-1193
(202) 939-9300

Within the American Council on Education, the Center for Adult Learning and Educational Credentials administers the National External Diploma Program, the GED Program, the Program on Noncollegiate Sponsored Instruction, the Credit by Examination Program, and the Military Evaluations Program.

DANTES Subject Standardized Tests

INTRODUCTION

The DANTES (Defense Activity for Non-Traditional Education Support) subject standardized tests are comprehensive college and graduate level examinations given by the Armed Forces, colleges and graduate schools as end-of-subject course evaluation final examinations or to obtain college equivalency credits in the various subject areas tested.

The DANTES Examination Program enables students to obtain college credit for what they have learned on the job, through self-study, personal interest, correspondence courses or by any other means. It is used by colleges and universities to award college credit to students who demonstrate that they know as much as students completing an equivalent college course. It is a cost-efficient, time-saving way for students to use their knowledge to accomplish their educational goals.

Most schools accept the American Council on Education (ACE) recommendations for the minimum score required and the amount of credit awarded, but not all schools do. Be sure to check the policy regarding the score level required for credit and the number of credits to be awarded.

Not all tests are accepted by all institutions. Even when a test is accepted by an institution, it may not be acceptable for every program at that institution. Before considering testing, ascertain the acceptability of a specific test for a particular course.

Colleges and universities that administer DANTES tests may administer them to any applicant – or they may administer the tests only to students registered at their institution. Decisions about who will be allowed to test are made by the school. Students should contact the test center to determine current policies and schedules for DANTES testing.

Colleges and universities authorized to administer DANTES tests usually do so throughout the calendar year. Each school sets its own fee for test administration and establishes its own testing schedule. Contact the representative at the administering school directly to make arrangements for testing.

Checklist

For Students

- ✓ Visit **www.getcollegecredit.com** to obtain a list of tests, fact sheets, test preparation materials, participating colleges and universities, and much more.
- ✓ Contact your school advisor to confirm that the DSST you selected will fit into your curriculum.
- ✓ Consult the ***DSST Candidate Information Bulletin*** for answers to specific questions.
- ✓ Contact the test site to schedule your test.
- ✓ Prepare for your examination by using the fact sheet as a guide.
- ✓ Take the test.

If you would like a score report sent to your college or university, it is a good idea to bring the four-digit code with you. You must write the DSST Test Center Code for that institution on your answer sheet at the time of testing. DSST Test Center Codes are noted in the DSST Participating Colleges and Universities listing on the Web site.

If you prefer to send a score report to an institution at a later date, there is a transcript fee of $20 for each transcript ordered.

Thomson Prometric
DSST Program
2000 Lenox Drive, Third Floor
Lawrenceville, NJ 08648

Toll-free: 877-471-9860
609-895-5011

E-mail: pnj-dsst@thomson.com

MAKING A COLLEGE DEGREE WITHIN YOUR REACH

Today, there are many educational alternatives to the classroom—you can learn from your job, your reading, your independent study, and special interests you pursue. You may already have learned the subject matter covered by some college-level courses.

The DSST Program is a nationally recognized testing program that gives you the opportunity to receive college credit for learning acquired outside the traditional college classroom. Colleges and universities throughout the United States administer the program, developed by Thomson Prometric, year-round. Annually, over 90,000 DSSTs are administered to individuals who are interested in continuing their education. Take advantage of the DSST testing program; it speeds the educational process and provides the flexibility adults need, making earning a degree more feasible.

Since requirements differ from college to college, please check with the credit-awarding institution before taking a DSST. More than 1,800 colleges and universities currently award credit for DSSTs, and the number is growing every day. You can choose from 37 test titles in the areas of Social Science, Business, Mathematics, Applied Technology, Humanities, and Physical Science. A brief description of each examination is found on the pages that follow.

Reach Your Career Goals Through DSSTs

Use DSSTs to help you earn your degree, get a promotion, or simply demonstrate that you have college-level knowledge in subjects relevant to your work.

Save Time...

You don't have to sit through classes when you have previously acquired the knowledge or experience for most of what is being taught and can learn the rest yourself. You might be able to bypass introductory-level courses in subject areas you already know.

Save Money...

DSSTs save you money because the classes you bypass by earning credit through the DSST Program are classes you won't have to pay for on your way to earning your degree. You can use the money instead to take more advanced courses that can be more challenging and rewarding.

Improve Your Chances for Admission to College

Each college has its own admission policies; however, having passing scores for DSSTs on your transcript can provide strong evidence of how well you can perform at the college level.

Gain Confidence Performing at a College Level

Many adults returning to college find that lack of confidence is often the greatest hurdle to overcome. Passing a DSST demonstrates your ability to perform on a college level.

Make Up for Courses You May Have Missed

You may be ready to graduate from college and find that you are a few credits short of earning your degree. By using semester breaks, vacation time, or leisure time to study independently, you can prepare to take one or more DSSTs, fulfill your academic requirements, and graduate on time.

If You Cannot Attend Regularly Scheduled Classes...

If your lifestyle or responsibilities prevent you from attending regularly scheduled classes, you can earn your college degree from a college offering an external degree program. The DSST Program allows you to earn your degree by study and experience outside the traditional classroom.

Many colleges and universities offer external degree or distance learning programs. For additional information, contact the college you plan to attend or:

Center for Lifelong Learning
American Council on Education
One DuPont Circle NW, Suite 250
Washington, DC 20036
202-939-9475
www.acenet.edu
(Select "Center for Lifelong Learning" under "Programs & Services" for more information)

Fact Sheets

For each test, there is a Fact Sheet that outlines the topics covered by each test and includes a list of sample questions, a list of recommended references of books that would be useful for review, and the number of credits awarded for a passing score as recommended by the American Council on Education (ACE). *Please note that some schools require scores that are higher than the minimum ACE-recommended passing score.* It is suggested that you check with your college or university to determine what score they require in order to earn credit. You can obtain Fact Sheets by:

- Downloading them from www.getcollegecredit.com
- E-mailing a request to pnj-dsst@thomson.com
- Completing a Candidate Publications Order Form

DSST Online Practice Tests

DSST online practice tests contain items that reflect a *partial range of difficulty* identified in the Content Outline section on each Fact Sheet. There is an online DSST Practice Test in the following categories:

- Mathematics
- Social Science
- Business
- Physical Science
- Applied Technology
- Humanities

Although the online DSST Practice Test questions do not indicate the full range of difficulty you would find in an actual DSST test, they will help you assess your knowledge level. Each online DSST Practice Test can be purchased by visiting www.getcollegecredit.com and clicking on DSST Practice Exams.

TAKING DSST EXAMINATIONS

Earning College Credit for DSST Examinations

To find out if the college of your choice awards credit for passing DSST scores, contact the admissions office or counseling and testing office. The college can also provide information on the scores required for awarding credit, the number of credit hours awarded, and any courses that can be bypassed with satisfactory scores.

It is important that you contact the institution of your choice as early as possible since credit-awarding policies differ among colleges and universities.

Where to Take DSSTs

DSSTs are administered at colleges and universities nationwide. Each location determines the frequency and scheduling of test administrations. To obtain the most current list of participating DSST colleges and universities:

- Visit and download the information from www.getcollegecredit.com
- E-mail pnj-dsst@thomson.com

Scheduling Your Examination

Please be aware that some colleges and universities provide DSST testing services to enrolled students only. After you have selected a college or university that administers DSSTs, you will need to contact them to schedule your test date.

The fee to take a DSST is $60 per test. This fee entitles you to two score reports after the test is scored. One will be sent directly to you and the other will be sent to the college or university that you designate on your answer sheet. You may pay the test fee with a certified check or U.S. money order made payable to Thomson Prometric or you may charge the test fee to your Visa, MasterCard or American Express credit card. Note: The credit card statement will reflect a charge from Thomson Prometric for all DSST examinations. *(Declined credit card charges will be assessed an additional $25 processing fee.)*

In addition, the test site may also require a test administration fee for each examination, to be paid directly to the institution. Contact the test site to determine its administration fee and payment policy.

Other Testing Arrangements

If you are unable to find a participating DSST college or university in your area, you may want to contact the testing office of a local accredited college or university to determine whether a representative from that office will agree to administer the test(s) for you.

The school's representative should then contact the DSST Program at 866-794-3497 to arrange for this administration. If you are unable to locate a test site, contact Thomson Prometric for assistance at pnj-dsst@thomson.com or 866-794-3497.

Testing Accommodations for Students with Disabilities

Thomson Prometric is committed to serving test takers with disabilities by providing services and reasonable testing accommodations as set forth in the provisions of the *Americans with Disabilities Act* (ADA). If you have a disability, as prescribed by the ADA, and require special testing services or arrangements, please contact the test administrator at the test site. You will be asked to submit to the test administrator documentation of your disability and your request for special accommodations. The test administrator will then forward your documentation along with your request for testing accommodations to Thomson Prometric for approval.

Please submit your request as far in advance of your test date as possible so that the necessary accommodations can be made. Only test takers with documented disabilities are eligible for special accommodations.

On the Day of the Examination

It is important to review this information and to have the correct identification present on the day of the examination:

- Arrive on time as a courtesy to the test administrator.
- Bring a valid form of government-issued identification that includes a current photo and your signature (acceptable documents include a driver's license, passport, state-issued identification card or military identification). *Anyone who fails to present valid identification will not be allowed to test.*
- Bring several No. 2 (soft-lead) sharpened pencils with good erasers, a watch, and a black pen if you will be writing an essay.
- Do not bring books or papers.
- Do not bring an alarm watch that beeps, a telephone, or a phone beeper into the testing room.
- The use of nonprogrammable calculators, slide rules, scratch paper and/or other materials is permitted for some of the tests.

DSST SCORING POLICIES

Your DSST examination scores are reported only to you, unless you request that they be sent elsewhere. If you want your scores sent to your college, you must provide the correct DSST code number of the school on your answer sheet at the time you take the test. See the *DSST Directory of Colleges and Universities* on the Web site www.getcollegecredit.com.

If your institution is not listed, contact Thomson Prometric at 866-794-3497 to establish a code number. (Some schools may require a student to be enrolled prior to receiving a score report.)

Receiving Your Score Report

Allow approximately four weeks after testing to receive your score report.

Calling DSST Customer Service before the required four-week score processing time has elapsed will not expedite the processing of your scores. Due to privacy and security requirements, scores will not be reported to students over the telephone under any circumstance.

Scoring of Principles of Public Speaking Speeches

The speech portion of the *Principles of Public Speaking* examination will be sent to speech raters who are faculty members at accredited colleges that currently teach or have previously taught the course. Scores for the *Principles of Public Speaking* examination are available six to eight weeks from receipt by Thomson Prometric. If you take the *Principles of Public Speaking* examination and fail (either the objective, speech portion, or both), you must follow the retesting policy waiting period of six months (180 days) before retaking the entire exam.

Essays

The essays for *Ethics in America* and *Technical Writing* are optional and thus are not scored by raters. The essays are forwarded to the college or university that you designate, along with your score report, for their use in determining the award of credit. Before taking the *Ethics in America* or *Technical Writing* examinations, check with your college or university to determine whether the essay is required.

NOTE: *Principles of Public Speaking* speech topic cassette tapes and essays are kept on file at Thomson Prometric for one year from the date of administration.

How to Get Transcripts

There is a $20 fee for each transcript you request. Payment must be in the form of a certified check, U.S. money order payable to Thomson Prometric, or credit card. Personal checks and debit cards are NOT an acceptable method of payment. One transcript may include scores for one or more examinations taken. To request a transcript, download the Transcript Order Form from www.getcollegecredit.com.

DESCRIPTION OF THE DSST EXAMINATIONS

Mathematics

• **Fundamentals of College Algebra** covers mathematical concepts such as fundamental algebraic operations; linear, absolute value; quadratic equations, inequalities, radials, exponents and logarithms, factoring polynomials and graphing. The use of a nonprogrammable, handheld calculator is permitted.

• **Principles of Statistics** tests the understanding of the various topics of statistics, both qualitatively and quantitatively, and the ability to apply statistical methods to solve a variety of problems. The topics included in this test are descriptive statistics; correlation and regression; probability; chance models and sampling and tests of significance. The use of a nonprogrammable, handheld calculator is permitted.

Social Science

• **Art of the Western World** deals with the history of art during the following periods: classical; Romanesque and Gothic; early Renaissance; high Renaissance, Baroque; rococo; neoclassicism and romanticism; realism, impressionism and post-impressionism; early twentieth century; and post-World War II.

• **Western Europe Since 1945** tests the knowledge of basic facts and terms and the understanding of concepts and principles related to the areas of the historical background of the aftermath of the Second World War and rebuilding of Europe; national political systems; issues and policies in Western European societies; European institutions and processes; and Europe's relations with the rest of the world.

• **An Introduction to the Modern Middle East** emphasizes core knowledge (including geography, Judaism, Christianity, Islam, ethnicity); nineteenth-century European impact; twentieth-century Western influences; World Wars I and II; new nations; social and cultural changes (1900-1960) and the Middle East from 1960 to present.

• **Human/Cultural Geography** includes the Earth and basic facts (coordinate systems, maps, physiography, atmosphere, soils and vegetation, water); culture and environment, spatial processes (social processes, modern economic systems, settlement patterns, political geography); and regional geography.

• **Rise and Fall of the Soviet Union** covers Russia under the Old Regime; the Revolutionary Period; New Economic Policy; Pre-war Stalinism; The Second World War; Post-war Stalinism; The Khrushchev Years; The Brezhnev Era; and reform and collapse.

• **A History of the Vietnam War** covers the history of the roots of the Vietnam War; the First Vietnam War (1946-1954); pre-war developments (1954-1963); American involvement in the Vietnam War; Tet (1968); Vietnamizing the War (1968-1973); Cambodia and Laos; peace; legacies and lessons.

• **The Civil War and Reconstruction** covers the Civil War from presecession (1861) through Reconstruction. It includes causes of the war; secession; Fort Sumter; the war in the east and in the west; major battles; the political situation; assassination of Lincoln; end of the Confederacy; and Reconstruction.

• **Foundations of Education** includes topics such as contemporary issues in education; past and current influences on education (philosophies, democratic ideals, social/economic influences); and the interrelationships between contemporary issues and influences.

• **Life-span Developmental Psychology** covers models and theories; methods of study; ethical issues; biological development; perception, learning and memory; cognition and language; social, emotional, and personality development; social behaviors, family life cycle, extrafamilial settings; singlehood and cohabitation; occupational development and retirement; adjustment to life stresses; and bereavement and loss.

• **Drug and Alcohol Abuse** includes such topics as drug use in society; classification of drugs; pharmacological principles; alcohol (types, effects of, alcoholism); general principles and use of sedative hypnotics, narcotic analgesics, stimulants, and hallucinogens; other drugs (inhalants, steroids); and prevention/treatment.

• **General Anthropology** deals with anthropology as a discipline; theoretical perspectives; physical anthropology; archaeology; social organization; economic organization; political organization; religion; and modernization and application of anthropology.

• **Introduction to Law Enforcement** includes topics such as history and professional movement of law enforcement; overview of the U.S. criminal justice system; police systems in the U.S.; police organization, management, and issues; and U.S. law and precedents.

• **Criminal Justice** deals with criminal behavior (crime in the U.S., theories of crime, types of crime); the criminal justice system (historical origins, legal foundations, due process); police; the court system (history and organization, adult court system, juvenile court, pre-trial and post-trial processes); and corrections.

• **Fundamentals of Counseling** covers historical development (significant influences and people); counselor roles and functions; the counseling relationship; and theoretical approaches to counseling.

Business

• **Principles of Finance** deals with financial statements and planning; time value of money; working capital management; valuation and characteristics; capital budgeting; cost of capital; risk and return; and international financial management. The use of a nonprogrammable, handheld calculator is permitted.

• **Principles of Financial Accounting** includes topics such as general concepts and principles, accounting cycle and classification; transaction analysis; accruals and deferrals; cash and internal control; current accounts; long- and short-term liabilities; capital stock; and financial statements. The use of a nonprogrammable, handheld calculator is permitted.

• **Human Resource Management** covers general employment issues; job analysis; training and development; performance appraisals; compensation issues; security issues; personnel legislation and regulation; labor relations and current issues; an overview of the Human Resource Management Field; Human Resource Planning; Staffing; training and development; compensation issues; safety and health; employee rights and discipline; employment law; labor relations and current issues and trends.

• **Organizational Behavior** deals with the study of organizational behavior (scientific approaches, research designs, data collection methods); individual processes and characteristics; interpersonal and group processes and characteristics; organizational processes and characteristics; and change and development processes.

• **Principles of Supervision** deals with the roles and responsibilities of the supervisor; management functions (planning, organization and staffing, directing at the supervisory level); and other topics (legal issues, stress management, union environments, quality concerns).

• **Business Law II** covers topics such as sales of goods; debtor and creditor relations; business organizations; property; and commercial paper.

• **Introduction to Computing** includes topics such as history and technological generations; hardware/software; applications to information technology; program development; data management; communications and connectivity; and computing and society. The use of a nonprogrammable, handheld calculator is permitted.

• **Management Information Systems** covers systems theory, analysis and design of systems, hardware and software; database management; telecommunications; management of the MIS functional area and informational support.

• **Introduction to Business** deals with economic issues affecting business; international business; government and business; forms of business ownership; small business, entrepreneurship and franchise; management process; human resource management; production and operations; marketing management; financial management; risk management and insurance; and management and information systems.

• **Money and Banking** covers the role and kinds of money; commercial banks and other financial intermediaries; central banking and the Federal Reserve system; money and macroeconomics activity; monetary policy in the U.S.; and the international monetary system.

• **Personal Finance** includes topics such as financial goals and values; budgeting; credit and debt; major purchases; taxes; insurance; investments; and retirement and estate planning. The use of auxiliary materials, such as calculators and slide rules, is NOT permitted.

• **Business Mathematics** deals with basic operations with integers, fractions, and decimals; round numbers; ratios; averages; business graphs; simple interest; compound interest and annuities; net pay and deductions; discounts and markups; depreciation and net worth; corporate securities; distribution of ownership; and stock and asset turnover.

Physical Science

• **Astronomy** covers the history of astronomy, celestial mechanics; celestial systems; astronomical instruments; the solar system; nature and evolution; the galaxy; the universe; determining astronomical distances; and life in the universe.

• **Here's to Your Health** covers mental health and behavior; human development and relationships; substance abuse; fitness and nutrition; risk factors, disease, and disease prevention; and safety, consumer awareness, and environmental concerns.

• **Environment and Humanity** deals with topics such as ecological concepts (ecosystems, global ecology, food chains and webs); environmental impacts; environmental management and conservation; and political processes and the future.

• **Principles of Physical Science I** includes physics: Newton's Laws of Motion; energy and momentum; thermodynamics; wave and optics; electricity and magnetism; chemistry: properties of matter; atomic theory and structure; and chemical reactions.

• **Physical Geology** covers Earth materials; igneous, sedimentary, and metamorphic rocks; surface processes (weathering, groundwater, glaciers, oceanic systems, deserts and winds, hydrologic cycle); internal Earth processes; and applications (mineral and energy resources, environmental geology).

Applied Technology

• **Technical Writing** covers topics such as theory and practice of technical writing; purpose, content, and organizational patterns of common types of technical documents; elements of various technical reports; and technical editing. Students have the option to write a short essay on one of the technical topics provided. Thomson Prometric will not score the essay; however, for determining the award of credit, a copy of the essay will be forwarded to the college or university you've designated along with the score report or transcript.

Humanities

• **Ethics in America** deals with ethical traditions (Greek views, Biblical traditions, moral law, consequential ethics, feminist ethics); ethical analysis of issues arising in interpersonal and personal-societal relationships and in professional and occupational roles; and relationships between ethical traditions and the ethical analysis of situations. Students have the option to write an essay to analyze a morally problematic situation in terms of issues relevant to a decision and arguments for alternative positions. Thomson Prometric will not score the essay; however, for determining the award of credit, a copy of the essay will be forwarded to the college or university you've designated along with the score report or transcript.

• **Introduction to World Religions** covers topics such as dimensions and approaches to religion; primal religions; Hinduism; Buddhism; Confucianism; Taoism; Judaism; Christianity; and Islam.

• **Principles of Public Speaking** consists of two parts: Part One consists of multiple-choice questions covering considerations of Principles of Public Speaking; audience analysis; purposes of speeches; structure/organization; content/supporting materials; research; language and style; delivery; communication apprehension; listening and feedback; and criticism and evaluation. Part Two requires the student to record an impromptu persuasive speech that will be scored.

FREQUENTLY ASKED QUESTIONS ABOUT DSSTs

In order to pass the test, must I study from one of the recommended references?

The recommended references are a listing of books that were being used as textbooks in college courses of the same or similar title at the time the test was developed. Appropriate textbooks for study are not limited to those listed in the fact sheet. If you wish to obtain study resources to prepare for the examination, you may reference either the current edition of the listed titles or textbooks currently used at a local college or university for the same class title. It is recommended that you reference more than one textbook on the topics outlined in the fact sheet. You should begin by checking textbook content against the content outline included on the front page of the DSST fact sheet before selecting textbooks that cover the text content from which to study. Textbooks may be found at the campus bookstore of a local college or university offering a course on the subject.

Is there a penalty for guessing on the tests?

There is no penalty for guessing on DSSTs, so you should mark an answer for each question.

How much time will I have to complete the test?

Many DSSTs can be completed within 90 minutes; however, additional time can be allowed if necessary.

What should I do if I find a test question irregularity?

Continue testing and then report the irregularity to the test administrator after the test. This may be done by asking that the test administrator note the irregularity on the Supervisor's Irregularity Report or you can write to Thomson Prometric, DSST Program, 2000 Lenox Drive, Third Floor, Lawrenceville, NJ 08648, and indicate the form and question number(s) or circumstances as well as your name and address.

When will I receive my score report?

Allow approximately four weeks from the date of testing to receive your score report. Allow six to eight weeks to receive a score report for the *Principles of Public Speaking* examination.

Will my test scores be released without my permission?

Your test score will not be released to anyone other than the school you designate on your answer sheet unless you write to us and ask us to send a transcript elsewhere. Instructions about how to do this can be found on your score report. Your scores may be used for research purposes, but individual scores are never made public nor are individuals identified if research findings are made public.

If I do not achieve a passing score on the test, how long must I wait until I can take the test again?

If you do not receive a score on the test that will enable you to obtain credit for the course, you may take the test again after six months (180 days). Please do not attempt to take the test before six months (180 days) have passed because you will receive a score report marked *invalid* and your test fee will not be refunded.

Can my test scores be canceled?

The test administrator is required to report any irregularities to Thomson Prometric. The consequence of bringing unauthorized materials into the testing room, or giving or receiving help, will be the forfeiture of your test fee and the invalidation of test scores. The DSST Program reserves the right to cancel scores and not issue score reports in such situations.

What can I do if I feel that my test scores were not accurately reported?

Thomson Prometric recognizes the extreme importance of test results to candidates and has a multi-step quality-control procedure to help ensure that reported scores are accurate. If you have reason to believe that your score(s) were not accurately reported, you may request to have your answer sheet reviewed and hand scored.

The fees for this service are:

- $20 fee if requested within six months of the test date
- $30 fee if requested more than six months from the test date
- $30 fee if a re-evaluation of the *Principles of Public Speaking* speech is requested

The fee for this service can be paid by credit card or by certified check or U.S. money order payable to Thomson Prometric. Submit your request for score verification along with the appropriate fee or credit card information (credit card number and expiration date) to Thomson Prometric, DSST Program, 2000 Lenox Drive, Third Floor, Lawrenceville, NJ 08648. Include your full name, the test title, the date you took the test, and your Social Security number. Candidates will be notified if a scoring discrepancy is discovered within four weeks of receipt of the request.

What does ACE recommendation mean?

The ACE recommendation is the minimum passing score recommended by the American Council on Education for any given test. It is equivalent to the average score of students in the DSST norming sample who received a grade of C for the course. Some schools require a score higher than the ACE recommendation.

Who is NLC?

National Learning Corporation (NLC) has been successfully preparing candidates for 40 years for over 5,000 exams. NLC publishes Passbook® study guides to help candidates prepare for all DANTES and CLEP exams and almost every other type of exam from high school through adult career.

Go to our website — www.passbooks.com — or call (800) 632-8888 for information about ordering our Passbooks.

To get detailed information on the DSST program and DSST preparation materials, visit www.getcollegecredit.com.

If you are interested in taking the DSST exams, call 877-471-9860 or e-mail pnj-dsst@thomson.com.

INTRODUCTION TO MANAGEMENT

DESCRIPTION OF THE TEST

The Introduction to Management examination covers the material that is usually taught in an introductory one-term course in the essentials of management and organization. The fact that such courses are offered by different types of institutions and in a number of fields other than business has been taken into account in the preparation of this examination. The test requires a knowledge of human resources and operational and functional aspects of management, but primary emphasis is placed on functional aspects of management.

The examination is 90 minutes long and includes approximately 100 multiple-choice questions to be answered in two separately timed 45-minute sections.

KNOWLEDGE AND SKILLS REQUIRED

The questions on the examination fall into four major categories as follows:

Approximate Percent of Examination

15% Manpower and Human Resources
- Personnel Administration
- Collecting Bargaining
- Human Relations and Motivation
- Manpower Development

15% Operational Aspects of Management
- Production Planning and Control
- PERT
- Quality Controls
- Data Processing and Computer Assistance
- Inventory Control

60% Functional Aspects of Management
- Planning
- Organizing
- Directing
- Controlling
- Authority
- Decision Making
- Organization Charts
- Leadership
- Structure
- Budgeting

10% Miscellaneous Aspects of Management
Historical Aspects of Management
Social Responsibilities of Business
Systems
Contingency Perspectives

Questions on the test require candidates to demonstrate the following abilities. Some questions may require more than one of the abilities.

- Specific factual knowledge, recall, and general understanding of purposes, functions, and techniques of management (about 10 percent of the examination)
- Understanding of and ability to associate the meaning of specific terminology with important management ideas, processes, techniques, concepts, and elements (about 40 percent of the examination)
- Understanding of theory and significant underlying assumptions, concepts, and limitations of management data, including a comprehension of the rationale of procedures, methods, and analyses (about 40 percent of the examination)
- Application of knowledge, general concepts, and principles to specific problems (about 10 percent of the examination)

SAMPLE QUESTIONS

The twenty-four (24) sample questions given here are similar to questions on the Introduction to Management examination, but they do not actually appear on the examination.

Before attempting to answer the sample questions, read all the information about the Introduction to Management examination on the preceding pages.

Try to answer correctly as many questions as possible within 25 minutes. Then compare your answers with the correct answers that are given on Page

DIRECTIONS: Each of the questions or incomplete statements below is followed by five suggested answers or completions. Select the one that is BEST in each case.

1. Which of the following words is NAOT logically related to the others? 1.____
   A. Planning B. Directing C. Producing
   D. Controlling E. Organizing

2. If a company increases its prices, the total revenue line on a break-even chart will 2.____
   A. shift upward over its entire length
   B. rise more steeply
   C. be unaffected
   D. rise less steeply
   E. shift downward over its entire length

3. Program Evaluation and Review Technique (PERT) is a system for 3.____
   A. developing the organization chart for a company
   B. scheduling and finding the critical path for production
   C. evaluating the performance of workers
   D. reviewing the overall financial condition of the company
   E. programming a computer

4. Which of the following is a CORRECT statement about controlling as a management function? 4.____
   A. It can be performed independently of planning.
   B. It is performed only by the controller of an organization.
   C. It is more prevalent in business than in government.
   D. It assumes a certain approach to motivating employees.
   E. To work effectively, it must be closely related to planning.

5. Which of the following statements about the "exception principle" is(are) CORRECT? 5.____
   I. It states that those who take exception to a directive should report the basis of their disagreement or objection to their superior immediately.
   II. It is concerned with correctly identifying what should be the logical "exceptions to every rule."
   III. It is an important control concept.

   The CORRECT answer is:
   A. I only
   B. II only
   C. III only
   D. I and III only
   E. II and III only

6. Decentralization tends to be encouraged by which of the following business trends? 6.____
   I. Product diversification
   II. Use of electronic computers
   III. Geographical expansion of operations

   The CORRECT answer is:
   A. I only
   B. II only
   C. III only
   D. I and III only
   E. II and III only

7. An effective program of work simplification would include all of the following steps EXCEPT: 7.____
   A. Begin the program by selecting a procedure wherein each unit of work is very time-consuming
   B. Break the total procedure down into its basic elements
   C. Question the elements for their essentiality
   D. Eliminate, simplify, rearrange, and combine the elements so that they will fit the new procedure
   E. Put the new method into practice with training and follow-up

8. Which of the following can be BEST determined by consulting an organization chart? 8.____
   A. The size of the company
   B. The relationships of people
   C. The nature of work performed
   D. The relationship of positions
   E. The quality of management of the firm

9. Which of the following BEST illustrates informal organization? 9.____
   A. Line authority, such as that of the field marshal and battalion commander in the military
   B. Staff authority, such as that of personnel or cost control in manufacturing
   C. Functional authority, such as corporate supervision of the legal aspect of pension plans in branch plants
   D. The acceptance of authority by subordinates
   E. Groupings based on such things as technical ability, seniority, and personal influence

10. The number of subordinates who directly report to a superior refers to the manager's 10.____
   A. span of control
   B. organizational role
   C. organizational structure
   D. chain of command
   E. general staff

11. In the complex role of a staff person, the personnel administrator has LEAST need of 11.____
   A. the capacity to appraise organizational performance against written statements of objectives and policies
   B. the ability to see the organization as a whole and each member in it as a total personality
   C. the ability to think clearly, practically, and with foresight
   D. the ability to command and to enforce rules and regulations among production employees
   E. skill in communication

12. The choice of organization structure to be used in a business should be 12.____
   A. made by mutual agreement among all of the people affected
   B. based on consideration of the type of organization structures used by competitors
   C. subject to definite and fixed rules
   D. based on the objectives of each individual business
   E. made by organization specialists rather than managers

13. Behaviorists have charged traditional managers with a lack of concern for 13.____
   A. formal organizational structure
   B. the quality of management decisions
   C. following organizational channels of communication
   D. the acceptability of management decisions to subordinates
   E. productivity through control

14. Which of the following typically requires more interpretation than the others? 14.____
A. A rule
B. A policy
C. A procedure
D. They require equal interpretation
E. If formulated properly, none should require interpretation

15. The concept of hierarchy of needs refers to which of the following? 15.____
A. Functional supervision
B. Unity of command
C. Line-staff conflict
D. Heuristic programming
E. None of the above

16. Recruitment of college graduates is usually the responsibility of 16.____
A. first-line supervisors
B. divisional managers
C. personnel managers
D. the placement office
E. section chiefs

17. Which of the following statements BEST shows an understanding of international management? 17.____
A. Practically none of the managerial attitudes, techniques, and approaches found successful in the United States can be used in other (comparative management) societies.
B. Although effective management plays an important role in the economic accomplishments of the United States, it has limited application in the developing countries of the world.
C. An understanding of the cultural differences of various countries and their impact on the management process is essential to success in a multinational firm.
D. Although some variations in cultures do exist, management fundamentals are universal and their application in different countries will generally be the same.
E. An effective manager in the United States who has a basic understanding of human relations can easily be transferred to another country and perform successfully.

18. Douglas McGregor's "Theory Y" provides management with which of the following? 18.____
A. An understanding of those assumptions of human behavior deduced from the concept of the "rational economic man"
B. A sound indication that production-centered supervisors are less effective than employee-centered supervisors
C. The idea that employees are most effectively motivated when guided by a clearly expressed system of rewards and penalties
D. A set of assumptions regarding human behavior implicit in much of the literature of traditional management
E. None of the above

19. Henry Gantt, Frank Gilbreth, and Federick Taylor are considered pioneers in the school of management generally referred to as the _____ school. 19.____
   A. management-process
   B. empirical
   C. scientific-management
   D. behaviorist
   E. social-system

20. Preparation of which of the following is the MOST logical first step in developing an annual operating plan? 20.____
   A. A sales forecast by product
   B. A production schedule by product
   C. A flow-of-funds statement by product
   D. A plant and equipment requirement forecast
   E. A pro forma income statement and balance sheet

21. A large span of control throughout an organization invariably results in 21.____
   A. low morale
   B. high morale
   C. an excess work load for each manager
   D. a flat (horizontal) organizational structure
   E. a tall (vertical) organizational structure

22. Which of the following generally provide the impetus for the organization of informal work groups? 22.____
   A. Contacts created by the work setting
   B. Individuals who oppose management
   C. Strong leaders who recruit members
   D. Individuals who know each other from nonwork activities
   E. Unions

23. Which of the following is an example of a line position in a manufacturing organization? 23.____
   A. A sales manager concerned with selling a product in a given territory
   B. The head of research and development concerned with new products
   C. The controller concerned with establishing budgets
   D. The personnel manager concerned with employing workers
   E. The quality control manager concerned with maintaining quality standards in a production plant

24. Operations-research groups should consist of 24.____
   A. mathematicians primarily
   B. statisticians primarily
   C. people trained in any quantitative discipline
   D. interdisciplinary teams
   E. middle and top management people

KEY (CORRECT ANSWERS)

1.	C	11.	D
2.	B	12.	D
3.	B	13.	D
4.	E	14.	B
5.	C	15.	E
6.	D	16.	C
7.	A	17.	C
8.	D	18.	E
9.	E	19.	C
10.	A	20.	A

21. D
22. A
23. A
24. D

HOW TO TAKE A TEST

You have studied long, hard and conscientiously.

With your official admission card in hand, and your heart pounding, you have been admitted to the examination room.

You note that there are several hundred other applicants in the examination room waiting to take the same test.

They all appear to be equally well prepared.

You know that nothing but your best effort will suffice. The "moment of truth" is at hand: you now have to demonstrate objectively, in writing, your knowledge of content and your understanding of subject matter.

You are fighting the most important battle of your life—to pass and/or score high on an examination which will determine your career and provide the economic basis for your livelihood.

What extra, special things should you know and should you do in taking the examination?

I. YOU MUST PASS AN EXAMINATION

A. WHAT EVERY CANDIDATE SHOULD KNOW

Examination applicants often ask us for help in preparing for the written test. What can I study in advance? What kinds of questions will be asked? How will the test be given? How will the papers be graded?

B. HOW ARE EXAMS DEVELOPED?

Examinations are carefully written by trained technicians who are specialists in the field known as "psychological measurement," in consultation with recognized authorities in the field of work that the test will cover. These experts recommend the subject matter areas or skills to be tested; only those knowledges or skills important to your success on the job are included. The most reliable books and source materials available are used as references. Together, the experts and technicians judge the difficulty level of the questions.

Test technicians know how to phrase questions so that the problem is clearly stated. Their ethics do not permit "trick" or "catch" questions. Questions may have been tried out on sample groups, or subjected to statistical analysis, to determine their usefulness.

Written tests are often used in combination with performance tests, ratings of training and experience, and oral interviews. All of these measures combine to form the best-known means of finding the right person for the right job.

II. HOW TO PASS THE WRITTEN TEST

A. BASIC STEPS

1) Study the announcement

How, then, can you know what subjects to study? Our best answer is: "Learn as much as possible about the class of positions for which you've applied." The exam will test the knowledge, skills and abilities needed to do the work.

Your most valuable source of information about the position you want is the official exam announcement. This announcement lists the training and experience qualifications. Check these standards and apply only if you come reasonably close to meeting them. Many jurisdictions preview the written test in the exam announcement by including a section called "Knowledge and Abilities Required," "Scope of the Examination," or some similar heading. Here you will find out specifically what fields will be tested.

2) Choose appropriate study materials

If the position for which you are applying is technical or advanced, you will read more advanced, specialized material. If you are already familiar with the basic principles of your field, elementary textbooks would waste your time. Concentrate on advanced textbooks and technical periodicals. Think through the concepts and review difficult problems in your field.

These are all general sources. You can get more ideas on your own initiative, following these leads. For example, training manuals and publications of the government agency which employs workers in your field can be useful, particularly for technical and professional positions. A letter or visit to the government department involved may result in more specific study suggestions, and certainly will provide you with a more definite idea of the exact nature of the position you are seeking.

3) Study this book!

III. KINDS OF TESTS

Tests are used for purposes other than measuring knowledge and ability to perform specified duties. For some positions, it is equally important to test ability to make adjustments to new situations or to profit from training. In others, basic mental abilities not dependent on information are essential. Questions which test these things may not appear as pertinent to the duties of the position as those which test for knowledge and information. Yet they are often highly important parts of a fair examination. For very general questions, it is almost impossible to help you direct your study efforts. What we can do is to point out some of the more common of these general abilities needed in public service positions and describe some typical questions.

1) General information

Broad, general information has been found useful for predicting job success in some kinds of work. This is tested in a variety of ways, from vocabulary lists to questions about current events. Basic background in some field of work, such as sociology or economics, may be sampled in a group of questions. Often these are principles which have become familiar to most persons through exposure rather than through formal training. It is difficult to advise you how to study for these questions; being alert to the world around you is our best suggestion.

2) Verbal ability

An example of an ability needed in many positions is verbal or language ability. Verbal ability is, in brief, the ability to use and understand words. Vocabulary and grammar tests are typical measures of this ability. Reading comprehension or paragraph interpretation questions are common in many kinds of civil service tests. You are given a paragraph of written material and asked to find its central meaning.

IV. KINDS OF QUESTIONS

1. Multiple-choice Questions

Most popular of the short-answer questions is the "multiple choice" or "best answer" question. It can be used, for example, to test for factual knowledge, ability to solve problems or judgment in meeting situations found at work.

A multiple-choice question is normally one of three types:

- It can begin with an incomplete statement followed by several possible endings. You are to find the one ending which best completes the statement, although some of the others may not be entirely wrong.
- It can also be a complete statement in the form of a question which is answered by choosing one of the statements listed.
- It can be in the form of a problem – again you select the best answer.

Here is an example of a multiple-choice question with a discussion which should give you some clues as to the method for choosing the right answer:

When an employee has a complaint about his assignment, the action which will best help him overcome his difficulty is to

A. discuss his difficulty with his coworkers
B. take the problem to the head of the organization
C. take the problem to the person who gave him the assignment
D. say nothing to anyone about his complaint

In answering this question, you should study each of the choices to find which is best. Consider choice "A" – Certainly an employee may discuss his complaint with fellow employees, but no change or improvement can result, and the complaint remains unresolved. Choice "B" is a poor choice since the head of the organization probably does not know what assignment you have been given, and taking your problem to him is known as "going over the head" of the supervisor. The supervisor, or person who made the assignment, is the person who can clarify it or correct any injustice. Choice "C" is, therefore, correct. To say nothing, as in choice "D," is unwise. Supervisors have and interest in knowing the problems employees are facing, and the employee is seeking a solution to his problem.

2. True/False

3. Matching Questions

Matching an answer from a column of choices within another column.

V. RECORDING YOUR ANSWERS

Computer terminals are used more and more today for many different kinds of exams.

For an examination with very few applicants, you may be told to record your answers in the test booklet itself. Separate answer sheets are much more common. If this separate answer sheet is to be scored by machine – and this is often the case – it is highly important that you mark your answers correctly in order to get credit.

VI. BEFORE THE TEST

YOUR PHYSICAL CONDITION IS IMPORTANT

If you are not well, you can't do your best work on tests. If you are half asleep, you can't do your best either. Here are some tips:

1) Get about the same amount of sleep you usually get. Don't stay up all night before the test, either partying or worrying—DON'T DO IT!
2) If you wear glasses, be sure to wear them when you go to take the test. This goes for hearing aids, too.
3) If you have any physical problems that may keep you from doing your best, be sure to tell the person giving the test. If you are sick or in poor health, you relay cannot do your best on any test. You can always come back and take the test some other time.

Common sense will help you find procedures to follow to get ready for an examination. Too many of us, however, overlook these sensible measures. Indeed, nervousness and fatigue have been found to be the most serious reasons why applicants fail to do their best on civil service tests. Here is a list of reminders:

- Begin your preparation early – Don't wait until the last minute to go scurrying around for books and materials or to find out what the position is all about.
- Prepare continuously – An hour a night for a week is better than an all-night cram session. This has been definitely established. What is more, a night a week for a month will return better dividends than crowding your study into a shorter period of time.
- Locate the place of the exam – You have been sent a notice telling you when and where to report for the examination. If the location is in a different town or otherwise unfamiliar to you, it would be well to inquire the best route and learn something about the building.
- Relax the night before the test – Allow your mind to rest. Do not study at all that night. Plan some mild recreation or diversion; then go to bed early and get a good night's sleep.
- Get up early enough to make a leisurely trip to the place for the test – This way unforeseen events, traffic snarls, unfamiliar buildings, etc. will not upset you.
- Dress comfortably – A written test is not a fashion show. You will be known by number and not by name, so wear something comfortable.
- Leave excess paraphernalia at home – Shopping bags and odd bundles will get in your way. You need bring only the items mentioned in the official notice you received; usually everything you need is provided. Do not bring reference books to the exam. They will only confuse those last minutes and be taken away from you when in the test room.

- Arrive somewhat ahead of time – If because of transportation schedules you must get there very early, bring a newspaper or magazine to take your mind off yourself while waiting.
- Locate the examination room – When you have found the proper room, you will be directed to the seat or part of the room where you will sit. Sometimes you are given a sheet of instructions to read while you are waiting. Do not fill out any forms until you are told to do so; just read them and be prepared.
- Relax and prepare to listen to the instructions
- If you have any physical problem that may keep you from doing your best, be sure to tell the test administrator. If you are sick or in poor health, you really cannot do your best on the exam. You can come back and take the test some other time.

VII. AT THE TEST

The day of the test is here and you have the test booklet in your hand. The temptation to get going is very strong. Caution! There is more to success than knowing the right answers. You must know how to identify your papers and understand variations in the type of short-answer question used in this particular examination. Follow these suggestions for maximum results from your efforts:

1) Cooperate with the monitor

The test administrator has a duty to create a situation in which you can be as much at ease as possible. He will give instructions, tell you when to begin, check to see that you are marking your answer sheet correctly, and so on. He is not there to guard you, although he will see that your competitors do not take unfair advantage. He wants to help you do your best.

2) Listen to all instructions

Don't jump the gun! Wait until you understand all directions. In most civil service tests you get more time than you need to answer the questions. So don't be in a hurry. Read each word of instructions until you clearly understand the meaning. Study the examples, listen to all announcements and follow directions. Ask questions if you do not understand what to do.

3) Identify your papers

Civil service exams are usually identified by number only. You will be assigned a number; you must not put your name on your test papers. Be sure to copy your number correctly. Since more than one exam may be given, copy your exact examination title.

4) Plan your time

Unless you are told that a test is a "speed" or "rate of work" test, speed itself is usually not important. Time enough to answer all the questions will be provided, but this does not mean that you have all day. An overall time limit has been set. Divide the total time (in minutes) by the number of questions to determine the approximate time you have for each question.

5) Do not linger over difficult questions

If you come across a difficult question, mark it with a paper clip (useful to have along) and come back to it when you have been through the booklet. One caution if you do this – be sure to skip a number on your answer sheet as well. Check often to be sure that you have not lost your place and that you are marking in the row numbered the same as the question you are answering.

6) Read the questions

Be sure you know what the question asks! Many capable people are unsuccessful because they failed to read the questions correctly.

7) Answer all questions

Unless you have been instructed that a penalty will be deducted for incorrect answers, it is better to guess than to omit a question.

8) Speed tests

It is often better NOT to guess on speed tests. It has been found that on timed tests people are tempted to spend the last few seconds before time is called in marking answers at random – without even reading them – in the hope of picking up a few extra points. To discourage this practice, the instructions may warn you that your score will be "corrected" for guessing. That is, a penalty will be applied. The incorrect answers will be deducted from the correct ones, or some other penalty formula will be used.

9) Review your answers

If you finish before time is called, go back to the questions you guessed or omitted to give them further thought. Review other answers if you have time.

10) Return your test materials

If you are ready to leave before others have finished or time is called, take ALL your materials to the monitor and leave quietly. Never take any test material with you. The monitor can discover whose papers are not complete, and taking a test booklet may be grounds for disqualification.

VIII. EXAMINATION TECHNIQUES

1) Read the general instructions carefully. These are usually printed on the first page of the exam booklet. As a rule, these instructions refer to the timing of the examination; the fact that you should not start work until the signal and must stop work at a signal, etc. If there are any special instructions, such as a choice of questions to be answered, make sure that you note this instruction carefully.

2) When you are ready to start work on the examination, that is as soon as the signal has been given, read the instructions to each question booklet, underline any key words or phrases, such as least, best, outline, describe and the like. In this way you will tend to answer as requested rather than discover on reviewing your paper that you listed without describing, that you selected the worst choice rather than the best choice, etc.

3) If the examination is of the objective or multiple-choice type – that is, each question will also give a series of possible answers: A, B, C or D, and you are called upon to select the best answer and write the letter next to that answer on your answer paper – it is advisable to start answering each question in turn. There may be anywhere from 50 to 100 such questions in the three or four hours allotted and you can see how much time would be taken if you read through all the questions before beginning to answer any. Furthermore, if you

come across a question or group of questions which you know would be difficult to answer, it would undoubtedly affect your handling of all the other questions.

4) If the examination is of the essay type and contains but a few questions, it is a moot point as to whether you should read all the questions before starting to answer any one. Of course, if you are given a choice – say five out of seven and the like – then it is essential to read all the questions so you can eliminate the two that are most difficult. If, however, you are asked to answer all the questions, there may be danger in trying to answer the easiest one first because you may find that you will spend too much time on it. The best technique is to answer the first question, then proceed to the second, etc.

5) Time your answers. Before the exam begins, write down the time it started, then add the time allowed for the examination and write down the time it must be completed, then divide the time available somewhat as follows:
   - If 3-1/2 hours are allowed, that would be 210 minutes. If you have 80 objective-type questions, that would be an average of 2-1/2 minutes per question. Allow yourself no more than 2 minutes per question, or a total of 160 minutes, which will permit about 50 minutes to review.
   - If for the time allotment of 210 minutes there are 7 essay questions to answer, that would average about 30 minutes a question. Give yourself only 25 minutes per question so that you have about 35 minutes to review.

6) The most important instruction is to read each question and make sure you know what is wanted. The second most important instruction is to time yourself properly so that you answer every question. The third most important instruction is to answer every question. Guess if you have to but include something for each question. Remember that you will receive no credit for a blank and will probably receive some credit if you write something in answer to an essay question. If you guess a letter – say "B" for a multiple-choice question – you may have guessed right. If you leave a blank as an answer to a multiple-choice question, the examiners may respect your feelings but it will not add a point to your score. Some exams may penalize you for wrong answers, so in such cases only, you may not want to guess unless you have some basis for your answer.

7) Suggestions
   a. Objective-type questions
      1. Examine the question booklet for proper sequence of pages and questions
      2. Read all instructions carefully
      3. Skip any question which seems too difficult; return to it after all other questions have been answered
      4. Apportion your time properly; do not spend too much time on any single question or group of questions
      5. Note and underline key words – all, most, fewest, least, best, worst, same, opposite, etc.
      6. Pay particular attention to negatives
      7. Note unusual option, e.g., unduly long, short, complex, different or similar in content to the body of the question
      8. Observe the use of "hedging" words – probably, may, most likely, etc.

9. Make sure that your answer is put next to the same number as the question
10. Do not second-guess unless you have good reason to believe the second answer is definitely more correct
11. Cross out original answer if you decide another answer is more accurate; do not erase until you are ready to hand your paper in
12. Answer all questions; guess unless instructed otherwise
13. Leave time for review

b. Essay questions

1. Read each question carefully
2. Determine exactly what is wanted. Underline key words or phrases.
3. Decide on outline or paragraph answer
4. Include many different points and elements unless asked to develop any one or two points or elements
5. Show impartiality by giving pros and cons unless directed to select one side only
6. Make and write down any assumptions you find necessary to answer the questions
7. Watch your English, grammar, punctuation and choice of words
8. Time your answers; don't crowd material

8) Answering the essay question

Most essay questions can be answered by framing the specific response around several key words or ideas. Here are a few such key words or ideas:

M's: manpower, materials, methods, money, management
P's: purpose, program, policy, plan, procedure, practice, problems, pitfalls, personnel, public relations

a. Six basic steps in handling problems:

1. Preliminary plan and background development
2. Collect information, data and facts
3. Analyze and interpret information, data and facts
4. Analyze and develop solutions as well as make recommendations
5. Prepare report and sell recommendations
6. Install recommendations and follow up effectiveness

b. Pitfalls to avoid

1. Taking things for granted – A statement of the situation does not necessarily imply that each of the elements is necessarily true; for example, a complaint may be invalid and biased so that all that can be taken for granted is that a complaint has been registered
2. Considering only one side of a situation – Wherever possible, indicate several alternatives and then point out the reasons you selected the best one
3. Failing to indicate follow up – Whenever your answer indicates action on your part, make certain that you will take proper follow-up action to see how successful your recommendations, procedures or actions turn out to be
4. Taking too long in answering any single question – Remember to time your answers properly

EXAMINATION SECTION

EXAMINATION SECTION

TEST 1

DIRECTIONS: Each question or incomplete statement is followed by several suggested answers or completions. Select the one that BEST answers the question or completes the statement. *PRINT THE LETTER OF THE CORRECT ANSWER IN THE SPACE AT THE RIGHT.*

1. Although some kinds of instructions are best put in written form, a supervisor can give many instructions verbally. 1.____
In which one of the following situations would verbal instructions be MOST suitable?
   A. Furnishing an employee with the details to be checked in doing a certain job
   B. Instructing an employee on the changes necessary to update the office manual used in your unit
   C. Informing a new employee where different kinds of supplies and equipment that he might need are kept
   D. Presenting an assignment to an employee who will be held accountable for following a series of steps

2. You may be asked to evaluate the organization structure of your unit. 2.____
Which one of the following questions would you NOT expect to take up in an evaluation of this kind?
   A. Is there an employee whose personal problems are interfering with his or her work?
   B. Is there an up-to-date job description for each position in this section?
   C. Are related operations and tasks grouped together and regularly assigned together?
   D. Are responsibilities divided as far as possible, and is this division clearly understood by all employees?

3. In order to distribute and schedule work fairly and efficiently, a supervisor may wish to make a work distribution study. A simple way of getting the information necessary for such a study is to have everyone for one week keep track of each task doe and the time spent on each. 3.____
Which one of the following situations showing up in such study would MOST clearly call for corrective action?
   A. The newest employee takes longer to do most tasks than do experienced employees.
   B. One difficult operation takes longer to do than most other operations carried out by the section.
   C. A particular employee is very frequently assigned tasks that are not similar and have no relationship to each other.
   D. The most highly skilled employee is often assigned the most difficult jobs.

4. The authority to carry out a job can be delegated to a subordinate, but the supervisor remains responsible for the work of the section as a whole. 4.____
As a supervisor, which of the following rules would be the BEST one for you to follow in view of the above statement?
   A. Avoid assigning important tasks to your subordinates, because you will be blamed if anything goes wrong
   B. Be sure each subordinate understands the specific job he has been assigned, and check at intervals to make sure assignments are done properly
   C. Assign several people to every important job so that responsibility will be spread out as much as possible
   D. Have an experienced subordinate check all work done by other employees so that there will be little chance of anything going wrong

5. The human tendency to resist change is often reflected in higher rates of turnover, absenteeism, and errors whenever an important change is made in an organization. Although psychologists do not fully understand the reasons why people resist change, they believe that the resistance stems from a threat to the individual's security, that it is a form of fear of the unknown. 5.____
In light of this statement, which one of the following approaches would probably be MOST effective in preparing employees for a change in procedure in their unit?
   A. Avoid letting employees know anything about the change until the last possible moment
   B. Sympathize with employees who resent the change and let them know you share their doubts and fears
   C. Promise the employees that if the change turns out to be a poor one, you will allow them to suggest a return to the old system
   D. Make sure that employees know the reasons for the change and are aware of the benefits that are expected from it

6. Each of the following methods of encouraging employee participation in work planning has been used effectively with different kinds and sizes of employee groups. 6.____
Which one of the following methods would be MOST suitable for a group of four technically skilled employees?
   A. Discussions between the supervisor and a representative of the group
   B. A suggestion program with semi-annual awards for outstanding suggestions
   C. A group discussion summoned whenever a major problem remains unsolved for more than a month
   D. Day-to-day exchange of information, opinions, and experience

7. Of the following, the MOST important reason why a supervisor is given the authority to tell subordinates what work they should do, how they should do it, and when it should be done is that usually 7.____
   A. most people will not work unless there is someone with authority standing over them

B. work is accomplished more effectively if the supervisor plans and coordinates it
C. when division of work is left up to subordinates, there is constant arguing, and very little work is accomplished
D. subordinates are not familiar with the tasks to be performed

8. Fatigue is a factor that affects productivity in all work situations. However, a brief rest period will ordinarily serve to restore a person from fatigue. 8.____
According to this statement, which one of the following techniques is MOST likely to reduce the impact of fatigue on overall productivity in a unit?
A. Scheduling several short breaks throughout the day
B. Allowing employees to go home early
C. Extending the lunch period an extra half hour
D. Rotating job assignments every few weeks

9. After giving a new task to an employee, it is a good idea for a supervisor to ask specific questions to make sure that the employee grasps the essentials of the task and sees how it can be carried out. Questions which ask the employee what he thinks or how he feels about an important aspect of the task are particularly effective. 9.____
Which one of the following questions is NOT the type of question which would be useful in the foregoing situation?
A. Do you feel there will be any trouble meeting the 4:30 deadline?
B. How do you feel about the kind of work we do here?
C. Do you think that combining those two steps will work all right?
D. Can you think of any additional equipment you may need for this process?

10. Of the following, the LEAST important reason for having a *continuous* training program is that 10.____
A. employees may forget procedures that they have already learned
B. employees may develop shortcuts on the job that result in inaccurate work
C. the job continue to change because of new procedures and equipment
D. training is one means of measuring effectiveness and productivity on the job

11. In training a new employee, it is usually advisable to break down the job into meaningful parts and have the new employee master one part before going on to the next. 11.____
Of the following, the BEST reason for using this technique is to
A. let the new employee know the reason for what he is doing and thus encourage him to remain in the unit
B. make the employee aware of the importance of the work and encourage him to work harder
C. show the employee that the work is easy so that he will be encouraged to work faster
D. make it more likely that the employee will experience success and will be encouraged to continue learning the job

12. You may occasionally find a serious error in the work of one of your subordinates. 12.____
Of the following, the BEST time to discuss such an error with an employee usually is
   A. immediately after the error is found
   B. after about two weeks, since you will also be able to point out some good things that the employee has accomplished
   C. when you have discovered a pattern of errors on the part of this employee so that he will not be able to dispute your criticism
   D. after the error results in a complaint by your own supervisor

13. For very important announcements to the staff, a supervisor should usually use both written and oral communications. For example, when a new procedure is to be introduced, the supervisor can more easily obtain the group's acceptance by giving his subordinates a rough draft of the new procedure and calling a meeting of all his subordinates. 13.____
The LEAST important benefit of this technique is that it will better enable the supervisor to
   A. explain why the change is necessary
   B. make adjustments in the new procedure to meet valid staff objections
   C. assign someone to carry out the new procedure
   D. answer questions about the new procedure

14. Assume that, while you are interviewing an individual to obtain information, the individual pauses in the middle of an answer. 14.____
The BEST of the following actions for you to take at that time is to
   A. correct any inaccuracies in what he has said
   B. remain silent until he continues
   C. explain your position on the matter being discussed
   D. explain that time is short and that he must complete his story quickly

15. When you are interviewing someone to obtain information, the BEST of the following reasons for you to repeat certain of his exact words is to 15.____
   A. assure him that appropriate action will be taken
   B. encourage him to switch to another topic of discussion
   C. assure him that you agree with his point of view
   D. encourage him to elaborate on a point he has made

16. Generally, when writing a letter, the use of precise words and concise sentences is 16.____
   A. *good*, because less time will be required to write the letter
   B. *bad*, because it is most likely that the reader will think the letter is unimportant and will not respond favorably
   C. *good*, because it is likely that your desired meaning will be conveyed to the reader
   D. *bad*, because your letter will be too brief to provide adequate information

17. In which of the following cases would it be MOST desirable to have two cards for one individual in a single alphabetic file? 17.____
The individual has
A. a hyphenated surname
B. two middle names
C. a first name with an unusual spelling
D. a compound first name

18. Of the following, it is MOST appropriate to use a form letter when it is necessary to answer many 18.____
A. requests or inquiries from a single individual
B. follow-up letters from individuals requesting additional information
C. request or inquiries about a single subject
D. complaints from individuals that they have been unable to obtain various types of information

19. Assume that you are asked to make up a budget for your section for the coming year, and you are told that the most important function of the budget is its "control function." 19.____
Of the following, "control" in this context implies MOST NEARLY that
A. you will probably be asked to justify expenditures in any category when it looks as though these expenditures are departing greatly from the amount budgeted
B. your section will probably not be allowed to spend more than the budgeted amount in any given category, although it is always permissible to spend less
C. your section will be required to spend the exact amount budgeted in every category
D. the budget will be filed in the Office of the Comptroller so that when a year is over the actual expenditures can be compared with the amounts in the budget

20. In writing a report, the practice of taking up the LEAST important points *first* and the most important points *last* is a 20.____
A. *good* technique, since the final points made in a report will make the greatest impression on the reader
B. *good* technique, since the material is presented in a more logical manner and will lead directly to the conclusions
C. *poor* technique, since the reader's time is wasted by having to review irrelevant information before finishing the report
D. *poor* technique, since it may cause the reader to lose interest in the report and arrive at incorrect conclusions about the report

21. Typically, when the technique of "supervision by results" is practiced, higher management sets down, either implicitly or explicitly, certain performance standards or goals that the subordinate is expected to meet. So long as these standards are met, management interferes very little. 21.____
The MOST likely result of the use of this technique is that it will

A. lead to ambiguity in terms of goals
B. be successful only to the extent that close direct supervision is practiced
C. make it possible to evaluate both employee and supervisory effectiveness
D. allow for complete dependence on the subordinate's part

22. When making written evaluations and reviews of the performance of subordinates, it is usually ADVISABLE to 22.____
A. avoid informing the employee of the evaluation if it is critical because it may create hard feelings
B. avoid informing the employee of the evaluation whether critical or favorable because it is tension-producing
C. to permit the employee to see the evaluation but not to discuss it with him because the supervisor cannot be certain where the discussion might lead
D. to discuss the evaluation openly with the employee because it helps the employee understand what is expected of him

23. There are a number of well-known and respected human relations principles that successful supervisors have been using for years in building good relationships with their employees. 23.____
Which of the following does NOT illustrate such a principle?
A. Give clear and complete instructions
B. Let each person know how he is getting along
C. Keep an open-door policy
D. Make all relationships personal ones

24. Assume that it is necessary for you to give an unpleasant assignment to one of your subordinates. You expect this employee to raise some objections to this assignment. 24.____
The MOST appropriate of the following actions for you to take FIRST is to issue the assignment
A. *orally*, with the further statement that you will not listen to any complaints
B. *in writing*, to forestall any complaints by the employee
C. *orally*, permitting the employee to express his feelings
D. *in writing*, with a note that any comments should be submitted in writing

25. Suppose you have just announced at a staff meeting with your subordinates that a radical reorganization of work will take place next week. Your subordinates at the meeting appear to be excited, tense, and worried. 25.____
Of the following, the BEST action for you to take at that time is to
A. schedule private conferences with each subordinate to obtain his reaction to the meeting
B. close the meeting and tell your subordinates to return immediately to their work assignments
C. give your subordinates some time to ask questions and discuss your announcement
D. insist that your subordinates do not discuss your announcement among themselves or with other members of the agency

KEY (CORRECT ANSWERS)

1. C
2. A
3. C
4. B
5. D

6. D
7. B
8. A
9. B
10. D

11. D
12. A
13. C
14. B
15. D

16. C
17. A
18. C
19. A
20. D

21. C
22. D
23. D
24. C
25. C

TEST 2

DIRECTIONS: Each question or incomplete statement is followed by several suggested answers or completions. Select the one that BEST answers the question or completes the statement. *PRINT THE LETTER OF THE CORRECT ANSWER IN THE SPACE AT THE RIGHT.*

1. Of the following, the BEST way for a supervisor to increase employees' interest in their work is to 1.____
   A. allow them to make as many decisions as possible
   B. demonstrate to them that he is as technically competent as they
   C. give each employee a difficult assignment
   D. promptly convey to them instructions from higher management

2. The one of the following which is LEAST important in maintaining a high level of productivity on the part of employees is the 2.____
   A. provision of optimum physical working conditions for employees
   B. strength of employees' aspirations for promotion
   C. anticipated satisfactions which employees hope to derive from their work
   D. employees' interest in their jobs

3. Of the following, the MAJOR advantage of group problem-solving, as compared to individual problem-solving, is that groups will more readily 3.____
   A. abide by their own decisions
   B. agree with agency management
   C. devise new policies and procedures
   D. reach conclusions sooner

4. The group problem-solving conference is a useful supervisory method for getting people to reach solutions to problems. 4.____
   Of the following, the reason that groups usually reach more realistic solutions than do individuals is that
   A. individuals, as a rule, take longer than do groups in reaching decisions and are, therefore, more likely to make an error
   B. bringing people together to let them confer impresses participants with the seriousness of problems
   C. groups are generally more concerned with the future in evaluating organizational problems
   D. the erroneous opinions of group members tend to be corrected by the other members

5. A competent supervisor should be able to distinguish between human and technical problems. 5.____
   Of the following, the MAJOR difference between such problems is that serious human problems, in comparison to ordinary technical problems
   A. are remedied more quickly
   B. involve a lesser need for diagnosis
   C. are more difficult to define
   D. become known through indications which are usually the actual problem

6. Of the following, the BEST justification for a public agency establishing an alcoholism program for its employees is that 6.____
   A. alcoholism has traditionally been looked upon with a certain amused tolerance by management and thereby ignored as a serious illness
   B. employees with drinking problems have twice as many on-the-job accidents, especially during the early years of the problem
   C. excessive use of alcohol is associated with personality instability hindering informal social relationships among peers and subordinates
   D. the agency's public reputation will suffer despite an employee's drinking problem being a personal matter of little public concern

7. Assume you are a manager and you find a group of maintenance employees assigned to your project drinking and playing cards for money in an incinerator room after their regular working hours. 7.____
   The one of the following actions it would be BEST for you to take is to
   A. suspend all employees immediately if there is no question in your mind as to the validity of the charges
   B. review the personnel records of those involved with the supervisor and make a joint decision on which employees should sustain penalties of loss of annual leave or fines
   C. ask the supervisor to interview each violator and submit written reports to you and thereafter consult with the supervisor about disciplinary actions
   D. deduct three days of annual leave from each employee involved if he pleads guilty in lieu of facing more serious charges

8. Assume that as a manager you must discipline a subordinate, but all of the pertinent facts necessary for a full determination of the appropriate action to take are not yet available. However, you fear that a delay in disciplinary action may damage the morale of other employees. 8.____
   The one of the following which is MOST appropriate for you to do in this matter is to
   A. take immediate disciplinary action as if all the pertinent facts were available
   B. wait until all pertinent facts are available before reaching a decision
   C. inform the subordinate that you know he is guilty, issue a stern warning, and then let him wait for your further action
   D. reduce the severity of the discipline appropriate for the violation

9. There are two standard dismissal procedures utilized by most public agencies. The first is the "open back door" policy, in which the decision of a supervisor in discharging an employee for reasons of inefficiency cannot be cancelled by the central personnel agency. The second is the "closed back door" policy, in which the central personnel agency can order the supervisor to restore the discharged employee to his position. 9.____
   Of the following, the major DISADVANTAGE of the "closed back door" policy as opposed to the "open back door" policy is that central personnel agencies are
   A. likely to approve the dismissal of employees when there is inadequate justification

B. likely to revoke dismissal actions out of sympathy for employees
C. less qualified than employing agencies to evaluate the efficiency of employees
D. easily influenced by political, religious, and racial factors

10. The one of the following for which a formal grievance-handling system is LEAST useful is in 10.____
A. reducing the frequency of employee complaints
B. diminishing the likelihood of arbitrary action by supervisors
C. providing an outlet for employee frustrations
D. bringing employee problems to the attention of higher management

11. The one of the following managers whose leadership style involves the GREATEST delegation of authority to subordinates is the one who presents to subordinates 11.____
A. his ideas and invites questions
B. his decision and persuades them to accept it
C. the problem, gets their suggestions, and makes his decision
D. a tentative decision which is subject to change

12. Which of the following is MOST likely to cause employee productivity standards to be set too high? 12.____
A. Standards of productivity are set by first-line supervisors rather than by higher level managers.
B. Employees' opinions about productivity standards are sought through written questionnaires.
C. Initial studies concerning productivity are conducted by staff specialists.
D. Ideal work conditions assumed in the productivity standards are lacking in actual operations.

13. The one of the following which states the MAIN value of an organization chart for a manager is that such charts show the 13.____
A. lines of formal authority
B. manner in which duties are performed by each employee
C. flow of work among employees on the same level
D. specific responsibilities of each position

14. Which of the following BEST names the usual role of a line unit with regard to the organization's programs? 14.____
A. Seeking publicity
B. Developing
C. Carrying out
D. Evaluating

15. Critics of promotion *from within* a public agency argue for hiring *from outside* the agency because they believe that promotion from within leads to 15.____
A. resentment and consequent weakened morale on the part of those not promoted
B. the perpetuation of outdated practices and policies
C. a more complex hiring procedure than hiring from outside the agency
D. problems of objectively appraising someone already in the organization

16. The one of the following management functions which usually can be handled MOST effectively by a committee is the 16.____
    A. settlement of interdepartmental disputes
    B. planning of routine work schedules
    C. dissemination of information
    D. assignment of personnel

17. Assume that you are serving on a committee which is considering proposals in order to recommend a new maintenance policy. After eliminating a number of proposals by unanimous consent, the committee is deadlocked on three proposals. 17.____
    The one of the following which is the BEST way for the committee to reach agreement on a proposal they could recommend is to
    A. consider and vote on each proposal separately by secret ballot
    B. examine and discuss the three proposals until the proponents of two of them are persuaded they are wrong
    C. reach a synthesis which incorporates the significant features of each proposals
    D. discuss the three proposals until the proponents of each one concede those aspects of the proposals about which there is disagreement

18. A commonly used training and development method for professional staff is the case method, which utilizes the description of a situation, real or simulated, to provide a common base for analysis, discussion, and problem-solving. 18.____
    Of the following, the MOST appropriate time to use the case method is when professional staff needs
    A. insight into their personality problems
    B. practice in applying management concepts to their own problems
    C. practical experience in the assignment of delegated responsibilities
    D. to know how to function in many different capacities

19. The incident process is a training and development method in which trainees are given a very brief statement of an event or o a situation presenting a job incident or an employee problem of special significance. 19.____
    Of the following, it is MOST appropriate to use the incident process when
    A. trainees need to learn to review and analyze facts before solving a problem
    B. there are a large number of trainees who require the same information
    C. there are too many trainees to carry on effective discussion
    D. trainees are not aware of the effect of their behavior on others

20. The one of the following types of information about which a clerical employee is usually LEAST concerned during the orientation process is 20.____
    A. his specific job duties
    B. where he will work
    C. his organization's history
    D. who his associates will be

21. The one of the following which is the MOST important limitation on the degree to which work should be broken down into specialized tasks is the point at which 21.____
    A. there ceases to be sufficient work of a specialized nature to occupy employees
    B. training costs equal the half-yearly savings derived from further specialization
    C. supervision of employees performing specialized tasks becomes more technical than supervision of general employees
    D. it becomes more difficult to replace the specialist than to replace the generalist who performs a complex set of functions

22. When a supervisor is asked for his opinion of the suitability for promotion of a subordinate, the supervisor is actually being asked to predict the subordinate's future behavior in a new role. 22.____
    Such a prediction is MOST likely to be accurate if the
    A. higher position is similar to the subordinate's current one
    B. higher position requires intangible personal qualities
    C. new position has had little personal association with the subordinate away from the job

23. In one form of the non-directive evaluation interview, the supervisor communicates his evaluation to the employee and then listens to the employee's response without making further suggestions. 23.____
    The one of the following which is the PRINCIPAL danger of this method of evaluation is that the employee is MOST likely to
    A. develop an indifferent attitude towards the supervisor
    B. fail to discover ways of improving his performance
    C. become resistant to change in the organization's structure
    D. place the blame for his shortcomings on his co-workers

24. In establishing rules for his subordinates, a superior should be PRIMARILY concerned with 24.____
    A. creating sufficient flexibility to allow for exceptions
    B. making employees aware of the reasons for the rules and the penalties for infractions
    C. establishing the strength of his own position in relation to his subordinates
    D. having his subordinates know that such rules will be imposed in a personal manner

25. The practice of conducting staff training sessions on a periodic basis is generally considered 25.____
    A. *poor*; it takes employees away from their work assignments
    B. *poor*; all staff training should be done on an individual basis
    C. *good*; it permits the regular introduction of new methods and techniques
    D. *good*; it ensures a high employee productivity rate

6 (#2)

KEY (CORRECT ANSWERS)

1.	A	11.	C
2.	A	12.	D
3.	A	13.	A
4.	D	14.	C
5.	C	15.	B
6.	B	16.	A
7.	C	17.	C
8.	B	18.	B
9.	C	19.	A
10.	A	20.	C

21. A
22. A
23. B
24. B
25. C

EXAMINATION SECTION

TEST 1

DIRECTIONS: Each question or incomplete statement is followed by several suggested answers or completions. Select the one that BEST answers the question or completes the statement. *PRINT THE LETTER OF THE CORRECT ANSWER IN THE SPACE AT THE RIGHT.*

1. Professional staff members in large organizations are sometimes frustrated by a lack of vital work-related information because of the failure of some middle-management supervisors to pass along unrestricted information from top management. 1.____
   All of the following are considered to be reasons for such failure to pass along information EXCEPT the supervisors'
   A. belief that information affecting procedures will be ignored unless they are present to supervise their subordinates
   B. fear that specific information will require explanation or justification
   C. inclination to regard the possession of information as a symbol of higher status
   D. tendency to treat information a private property

2. Increasingly in government, employees' records are being handled by automated data processing systems. However, employees frequently doubt a computer's ability to handle their records properly. 2.____
   Which of the following is the BEST way for management to overcome such doubts?
   A. Conduct a public relations campaign to explain the savings certain to result from the use of computers
   B. Use automated data processing equipment made by the firm which has the best repair facilities in the industry
   C. Maintain a clerical force to spot check on the accuracy of the computer's recordkeeping
   D. Establish automated data processing systems that are objective, impartial, and take into account individual factors as far as possible

3. Some management experts question the usefulness of offering cash to individual employees for their suggestions. 3.____
   Which of the following reasons for opposing cash awards is MOST valid?
   A. Emphasis on individual gain deters cooperative effort.
   B. Money spent on evaluating suggestions may outweigh the value of the suggestions.
   C. Awards encourage employees to think about unusual methods of doing work.
   D. Suggestions too technical for ordinary evaluation are usually presented.

4. The use of outside consultants, rather than regular staff, in studying and recommending improvements in the operations of public agencies has been criticized.
Of the following, the BEST argument in favor of using regular staff is that such staff can better perform the work because they 4.____
   A. are more knowledgeable about operations and problems
   B. can more easily be organized into teams consisting of technical specialists
   C. may wish to gain additional professional experience
   D. will provide reports which will be more interesting to the public since they are more experienced

5. One approach to organizational problem-solving is to have all problem-solving authority centralized at the top of the organization.
However, from the viewpoint of providing maximum service to the public, this practice is UNWISE chiefly because it 5.____
   A. reduces the responsibility of the decision-makers
   B. produces delays
   C. reduces internal communications
   D. requires specialists

6. Research has shown that problem-solving efficiency is optimal when the motivation of the problem-solver is at a moderate rather than an extreme level.
Of the following, probably the CHIEF reason for this is that the problem-solver 6.____
   A. will cause confusion among his subordinates when his motivation is too high
   B. must avoid alternate solutions that tend to lead him up blind alleys
   C. can devote his attention to both the immediate problem as well as to other relevant problems in the general area
   D. must feel the need to solve the problem but not so urgently as to direct all his attention to the need and none to the means of solution

7. Don't be afraid to make mistakes. Many organizations are paralyzed from the fear of making mistakes. As a result, they don't do the things they should; they don't try new and different ideas.
For the effective supervisor, the MOST valid implication of this statement is that 7.____
   A. mistakes should not be encouraged, but there are some unavoidable risks in decision-making
   B. mistakes which stem from trying new and different ideas are usually not serious
   C. the possibility of doing things wrong is limited by one's organizational position
   D. the fear of making mistakes will prevent future errors

8. The duties of an employee under your supervision may be either routine, problem-solving, innovative, or creative.
Which of the following BEST describes duties which are both innovative and creative? 8.____

A. Checking to make sure that work is done properly
B. Applying principles in a practical matter
C. Developing new and better methods of meeting goals
D. Working at two or more jobs at the same time

9. According to modern management theory, a supervisor who uses as little authority as possible and as much as is necessary would be considered to be using a mode that is 9.____
   A. autocratic B. inappropriate
   C. participative D. directive

10. Delegation involves establishing and maintaining effective working arrangements between a supervisor and the persons who report to him. 10.____
    Delegation is MOST likely to have taken place when the
    A. entire staff openly discusses common problems in order to reach solutions satisfactory to the supervisor
    B. performance of specified work is entrusted to a capable person, and the expected results are mutually understood
    C. persons assigned to properly accomplish work are carefully evaluated and given a chance to explain shortcomings
    D. supervisor provides specific written instructions in order to prevent anxiety on the part of inexperienced persons

11. Supervisors often not aware of the effect that their behavior has on their subordinates. 11.____
    The one of the following training methods which would be BEST for changing such supervisory behavior is _____ training.
    A. essential skills B. off-the-job
    C. sensitivity D. developmental

12. A supervisor, in his role as a trainer, may have to decide on the length and frequency of training sessions. 12.___
    When the material to be taught is new, difficult, and lengthy, the trainer should be guided by the principle that for BEST results in such circumstances, sessions should be
    A. longer, relatively fewer in number, and held on successive days
    B. shorter, relatively greater in number, and spaced at intervals of several days
    C. of average length, relatively fewer in number, and held at intermittent intervals
    D. of random length and frequency, but spaced at fixed intervals

13. Employee training which is based on realistic simulation, sometimes known as *game play* or *role play*, is sometimes preferable to learning from actual experience on the job. 13.____
    Which of the following is NOT a correct statement concerning the value of simulation to trainees?

A. Simulation allows for practice in decision-making without any need for subsequent discussion.
B. Simulation is intrinsically motivating because it offers a variety of challenges.
C. Compared to other, more traditional training techniques, simulation is dynamic.
D. The simulation environment is nonpunitive as compared to real life.

14. Programmed instruction as a method of training has all of the following advantages EXCEPT: 14.____
A. Learning is accomplished in an optimum sequence of distinct steps.
B. Trainees have wide latitude in deciding what is to be learned within each program.
C. The trainee takes an active part in the learning process.
D. The trainee receives immediate knowledge of the results of his response.

15. In a work-study program, trainees were required to submit weekly written performance reports in order to insure that work assignments fulfilled the program objectives. 15.____
Such reports would also assist the administrator of the work-study program PRIMARILY to
A. eliminate personal counseling for the trainees
B. identify problems requiring prompt resolution
C. reduce the amount of clerical work for all concerned
D. estimate the rate at which budgeted funds are being expended

16. Which of the following would be MOST useful in order to avoid misunderstanding when preparing correspondence or reports? 16.____
A. Use vocabulary which is at an elementary level
B. Present each sentence as an individual paragraph
C. Have someone other than the writer read the material for clarity
D. Use general words which are open to interpretation

17. Which of the following supervisory methods would be MOST likely to train subordinates to give a prompt response to memoranda in an organizational setting where most transactions are informal? 17.____
A. Issue a written directive setting forth a schedule of strict deadlines
B. Let it be known, informally, that those who respond promptly will be rewarded
C. Follow up each memorandum by a personal inquiry regarding the receiver's reaction to it
D. Direct subordinates to furnish a precise explanation for ignoring memos

18. Conferences may fail for a number of reasons. Still, a conference that is an apparent failure may have some benefit. 18.____
Which of the following would LEAST likely be such a benefit?
It may
A. increase for most participants their possessiveness about information they have

B. produce a climate of good will and trust among many of the participants
C. provide most participants with an opportunity to learn things about the others
D. serve as a unifying force to keep most of the individuals functioning as a group

19. Assume that you have been assigned to study and suggest improvements in an operating unit of a delegate agency whose staff has become overwhelmed with problems, has had inadequate resources, and has become accustomed to things getting worse. The staff is indifferent to cooperating with you because they see no hope of improvement. 19.____
Which of the following steps would be LEAST useful in carrying out your assignment?
A. Encourage the entire staff to make suggestions to you for change
B. Inform the staff that management is somewhat dissatisfied with their performance
C. Let staff know that you are fully aware of their problems and stresses
D. Look for those problem area where changes can be made quickly

20. Which of the following statements about employer-employee relations is NOT considered to be correct by leading managerial experts? 20.____
A. An important factor in good employer-employee relations is treating workers respectfully.
B. Employer-employee relations are profoundly influenced by the fundamentals of human nature.
C. Good employer-employee relations must stem from top management and reach downward.
D. Employee unions are usually a major obstacle to establishing good employer-employee relations.

21. In connection with labor relations, the term *management rights* GENERALLY refers to 21.____
A. a managerial review system in a grievance system
B. statutory prohibitions that bar monetary negotiations
C. the impact of collective bargaining on government
D. those subjects which management considers to be non-negotiable

22. Barriers may exist to the utilization of women in higher level positions. Some of these barriers are attitudinal in nature. 22.____
Which of the following is MOST clearly attitudinal in nature?
A. Advancement opportunities which are vertical in nature and thus require seniority
B. Experience which is inadequate or irrelevant to the needs of a dynamic and progressive organization
C. Inadequate means of early identification of employees with talent and potential for advancement
D. Lack of self-confidence on the part of some women concerning their ability to handle a higher position

23. Because a reader reacts to the meaning he associates with a word, we can neve be sure what emotional impact a word may carry or how it may affect our readers. 23.____
The MOST logical implication of this statement for employees who correspond with members of the public is that
   A. a writer should try to select a neutral word that will not bias his writing by its hidden emotional meaning
   B. simple language should be used in writing letters denying requests so that readers are not upset by the denial
   C. every writer should adopt a writing style which he finds natural and easy
   D. whenever there is doubt as to how a word is defined, the dictionary should be consulted

24. A public information program should be based on clear information about the nature of actual public knowledge and opinion. One way of learning about the views of the public is through the use of questionnaires. 24.____
Which of the following is of LEAST importance in designing a questionnaire?
   A. A respondent should be asked for his name and address.
   B. A respondent should be asked to choose from among several statements the one which expresses his views.
   C. Questions should ask for responses in a form suitable for processing.
   D. Questions should be stated in familiar language.

25. Assume that you have accepted an invitation to speak before an interested group about a problem. You have brought with you for distribution a number of booklets and other informational material. 25.____
Of the following, which would be the BEST way to use this material?
   A. Distribute it before you begin talking so that the audience may read it at their leisure.
   B. Distribute it during your talk to increase the likelihood that it will be read.
   C. Hold it until the end of your talk, then announce that those who wish may take or examine the material.
   D. Before starting the talk, leave it on a table in the back of the room so that people may pick it up as they enter.

KEY (CORRECT ANSWERS)

1. A
2. D
3. A
4. A
5. B

6. D
7. A
8. C
9. C
10. B

11. C
12. B
13. A
14. B
15. B

16. C
17. C
18. A
19. B
20. D

21. D
22. D
23. A
24. A
25. C

TEST 2

DIRECTIONS: Each question or incomplete statement is followed by several suggested answers or completions. Select the one that BEST answers the question or completes the statement. *PRINT THE LETTER OF THE CORRECT ANSWER IN THE SPACE AT THE RIGHT.*

1. Of the following, the FIRST step in planning an operation is to 1.____
   A. obtain relevant information
   B. identify the goal to be achieved
   C. consider possible alternatives
   D. make necessary assignments

2. A supervisor who is extremely busy performing routine tasks is MOST likely making INCORRECT use of what basic principle of supervision? 2.____
   A. Homogeneous Assignment
   B. Span of Control
   C. Work Distribution
   D. Delegation of Authority

3. Controls help supervisors to obtain information from which they can determine whether their staffs are achieving planned goals. 3.____
   Which one of the following would be LEAST useful as a control device?
   A. Employee diaries
   B. Organization charts
   C. Periodic inspections
   D. Progress charts

4. A certain employee has difficulty in effectively performing a particular portion of his routine assignments, but his overall productivity is average. 4.____
   As the direct supervisor of his individual, your BEST course of action would be to
   A. attempt to develop the man's capacity to execute the problematic facets of his assignments
   B. diversify the employee's work assignments in order to build up his confidence
   C. reassign the man to less difficult tasks
   D. request in a private conversation that the employee improve his work output

5. A supervisor who uses persuasion as a means of supervising a unit would GENERALLY also use which of the following practices to supervise his unit? 5.____
   A. Supervise and control the staff with an authoritative attitude to indicate that he is a *take-charge* individual
   B. Make significant changes in the organizational operations so as to improve job efficiency
   C. Remove major communication barriers between himself, subordinates, and management
   D. Supervise everyday operations while being mindful of the problems of his subordinates

6. Whenever a supervisor in charge of a unit delegate a routine task to a capable subordinate, he tells him exactly how to do it. 6.____

This practice is GENERALLY
A. *desirable*, chiefly because good supervisors should be aware of the traits of their subordinates and delegate responsibilities to them accordingly
B. *undesirable*, chiefly because only non-routine tasks should be delegated
C. *desirable*, chiefly because a supervisor should frequently test the willingness of his subordinates to perform ordinary tasks
D. *undesirable*, chiefly because a capable subordinate should usually be allowed to exercise his own discretion in doing a routine job

7. The one of the following activities through which a supervisor BEST demonstrates leadership ability is by 7.____
A. arranging periodic staff meetings in order to keep his subordinates informed about professional developments in the field
B. frequently issuing definite orders and directives which will lessen the need for subordinates to make decisions in handling any tasks assigned to them
C. devoting the major part of his time to supervising subordinates so as to simulate continuous improvement
D. setting aside time for self-development and research so as to improve the skills, techniques, and procedures of his unit

8. The following three statements relate to the supervision of employees: 8.____
I. The assignment of difficult tasks that offer a challenge is more conducive to good morale than the assignment of easy tasks.
II. The same general principles of supervision that apply to men are equally applicable to women.
III. The best retraining program should cover all phases of an employee's work in a general manner.
Which of the following choices list ALL of the above statements that are generally correct?
A. II, III B. I C. I, II D. I, II, III

9. Which of the following examples BEST illustrates the application of the *exception principle* as a supervisory technique? 9.____
A. A complex job is divided among several employees who work simultaneously to complete the whole job in a shorter time.
B. An employee is required to complete any task delegated to him to such an extent that nothing is left for the superior who delegated the task except to approve it.
C. A superior delegates responsibility to a subordinate but retains authority to make the final decisions.
D. A superior delegates all work possible to his subordinates and retains that which requires his personal attention or performance

10. Assume that you are a supervisor. Your immediate superior frequently gives orders to your subordinates without your knowledge. 10.____
Of the following, the MOST direct and effective way for you to handle this problem is to

A. tell our subordinates to take orders only from you
B. submit a report to higher authority in which you cite specific instances
C. discuss it with your immediate superior
D. find out to what extent your authority and prestige as a supervisor have been affected

11. In an agency which has as its primary purpose the protection of the public against fraudulent business practices, which of the following would GENERALLY be considered an *auxiliary* or *staff* rather than a *line* function? 11.____
A. Interviewing victims of frauds and advising them about their legal remedies
B. Daily activities directed toward prevention of fraudulent business practices
C. Keeping records and statistics about business violations reported and corrected
D. Follow-up inspections by investigators after corrective action has been taken

12. A supervisor can MOST effectively reduce the spread of false rumors through the *grapevine* by 12.____
A. identifying and disciplining any subordinate responsible for initiating such rumors
B. keeping his subordinates informed as much as possible about matters affecting them
C. denying false rumors which might tend to lower staff morale and productivity
D. making sure confidential matters are kept secure from access by unauthorized employees

13. A supervisor has tried to learn about the background, education, and family relationships of his subordinates through observation, personal contact, and inspection of their personnel records. 13.____
These supervisor actions are GENERALLY
A. *inadvisable*, chiefly because they may lead to charges of favoritism
B. *advisable*, chiefly because they may make him more popular with his subordinates
C. *inadvisable*, chiefly because his efforts may be regarded as an invasion of privacy
D. *advisable*, chiefly because the information may enable him to develop better understanding of each of his subordinates

14. In an emergency situation, when action must be taken immediately, it is BEST for the supervisor to give orders in the form of 14.____
A. direct commands which are brief and precise
B. requests, so that his subordinates will not become alarmed
C. suggestions which offer alternative courses of action
D. implied directives, so that his subordinates may use their judgment in carrying them out

15. When demonstrating a new and complex procedure to a group of subordinates, it is ESSENTIAL that a supervisor 15.____
    A. go slowly and repeat the steps involved at least once
    B. show the employees common errors and the consequences of such errors
    C. go through the process at the usual speed so that the employees can see the rate at which they should work
    D. distribute summaries of the procedure during the demonstration and instruct his subordinates to refer to them afterwards

16. After a procedures manual has been written and distributed, 16.____
    A. continuous maintenance work is necessary to keep the manual current
    B. it is best to issue new manuals rather than make changes in the original manual
    C. no changes should be necessary
    D. only major changes should be considered

17. Of the following, the MOST important criterion of effective report writing is 17.____
    A. eloquence of writing style
    B. the use of technical language
    C. to be brief and to the point
    D. to cover all details

18. The use of electronic data processing 18.____
    A. has proven unsuccessful in most organizations
    B. has unquestionable advantages for all organizations
    C. is unnecessary in most organizations
    D. should be decided upon only after careful feasibility studies by individual organizations

19. The PRIMARY purpose of work measurement is to 19.____
    A. design and install a wage incentive program
    B. determine who should be promoted
    C. establish a yardstick to determine extent of progress
    D. set up a spirit of competition among employee

20. The action which is MOST effective in gaining acceptance of a study by the agency which is being studied is 20.____
    A. a directive from the agency head to install a study based on recommendations included in a report
    B. a lecture-type presentation following approval of the procedure
    C. a written procedure in narrative form covering the proposed system with visual presentations and discussions
    D. procedural charts showing the *before* situation, forms, steps, etc., to the employees affected

21. Which organization principle is MOST closely related to procedural analysis and improvement? 21.____
   A. Duplication, overlapping, and conflict should be eliminated.
   B. Managerial authority should be clearly defined.
   C. The objectives of the organization should be clearly defined.
   D. Top management should be freed of burdensome detail.

22. Which one of the following is the MAJOR objective of operational audits? 22.____
   A. Detecting fraud
   B. Determining organization problems
   C. Determining the number of personnel needed
   D. Recommending opportunities for improving operating and management practices

23. Of the following, the formalization of organization structure is BEST achieved by 23.____
   A. a narrative description of the plan of organization
   B. functional charts
   C. job descriptions together with organization charts
   D. multi-flow charts

24. Budget planning is MOST useful when it achieves 24.____
   A. cost control
   B. forecast of receipts
   C. performance review
   D. personnel reduction

25. GENERALLY, in applying the principle of delegation in dealing with subordinates, a supervisor 25.____
   A. allows his subordinates to set up work goals and to fix the limits within which they can work
   B. allows his subordinates to set up work goals and then gives detailed orders as to how they are to be achieved
   C. makes relatively few decisions by himself and frames his orders in broad, general terms
   D. provides externalized motivation for his subordinate

KEY (CORRECT ANSWERS)

1. B
2. D
3. B
4. A
5. D

6. D
7. C
8. C
9. D
10. C

11. C
12. B
13. D
14. A
15. A

16. A
17. C
18. D
19. C
20. C

21. A
22. D
23. C
24. A
25. C

EXAMINATION SECTION

TEST 1

DIRECTIONS: Each question or incomplete statement is followed by several suggested answers or completions. Select the one that BEST answers the question or completes the statement. *PRINT THE LETTER OF THE CORRECT ANSWER IN THE SPACE AT THE RIGHT.*

1. A management approach widely used today is based on the belief that decisions should be made and actions should be taken by managers closest to the organization's problems. 1.____
This style of management is MOST appropriately called _____ management.
   A. scientific
   B. means-end
   C. decentralized
   D. internal process

2. As contrasted with tall organization structures with narrow spans of control, flat organization structures with wide spans of control MOST usually provide 2.____
   A. fast communication and information flows
   B. more levels in the organizational hierarchy
   C. fewer workers reporting to supervisors
   D. lower motivation because of tighter control standards

3. Use of the systems approach is MOST likely to lead to 3.____
   A. consideration of the impact on the whole organization of actions taken in any part of that organization
   B. the placing of restrictions on departmental activity
   C. use of mathematical models to suboptimize production
   D. consideration of the activities of each unit of an organization as a totality without regard to the remainder of the organization

4. An administrator, with overall responsibility for all administrative operations in a large operating agency, is considering organizing the agency's personnel office around either of the following two alternative concepts: 4.____
Alternative I: A corps of specialists for each branch of personnel subject matter, whose skills, counsel, or work products are coordinated only by the agency personnel officer
Alternative II: A crew of so-called *personnel generalists*, who individually work with particular segments of the organization but deal with all subspecialties of the personnel function
The one of the following which MOST tends to be a DRAWBACK of Alternative I, as compared with Alternative II, is that
   A. training and employee relations work call for education, interests, and talents that differ from those required for classification and compensation work
   B. personnel office staff may develop only superficial familiarity with the specialized areas to which they have been assigned

C. supervisors may fail to get continuing overall personnel advice on an integrated basis
D. the personnel specialists are likely to become so interested in and identified with the operating view as to particular cases that they lose their professional objectivity and become merely advocates of what some supervisor wants

5. The matrix summary or decision matrix is a useful tool for making choices. Its effectiveness is MOST dependent upon the user's ability to 5.____
A. write a computer program (Fortran or Cobol)
B. assign weights representing the relative importance of the objectives
C. solve a set of two equations with two unknowns
D. work with matrix algebra

6. An organizational form which is set up only on an *ad hoc* basis to meet specific goals is said PRIMARILY to use 6.____
A. clean break departmentation
B. matrix or task force organization
C. scalar specialization
D. geographic or area-wide decentralization

7. The concept of job enlargement would LEAST properly be implemented by 7.____
A. permitting workers to follow through on tasks or projects from start to finish
B. delegating the maximum authority possible for decision-making to lower levels in the hierarchy
C. maximizing the number of professional classes in the classification plan
D. training employees to grow beyond whatever tasks they have been performing

8. As used in the area of admission, the principle of *unity of command* MOST specifically means that 8.____
A. an individual should report to only one superior for any single activity
B. individuals make better decisions than do committees
C. in large organizations, chains of command are normally too long
D. an individual should not supervise over five subordinates

9. The method of operations research, statistical decision-making, and linear programming have been referred to as the tool kit of the manager. Utilization of these tools is LEAST useful in the performance of which of the following functions? 9.____
A. Elimination of the need for using judgment when making decisions
B. Facilitation of decision-making without the need for sub-optimization
C. Quantifying problems for management study
D. Research and analysis of management operations

10. When acting in their respective managerial capacities, the chief executive officer and the office supervisor both perform the fundamental functions of management. 10.____
Of the following differences between the two, the one which is generally considered to be the LEAST significant is the
   A. breadth of the objectives
   B. complexity of measuring actual efficiency of performance
   C. number of decisions made
   D. organizational relationships affected by actions taken

11. The ability of operations researchers to solve complicated problems rests on their use of models. 11.____
These models can BEST be described as
   A. mathematical statements of the problem
   B. physical constructs that simulate a work layout
   C. toy-like representations of employees in work environments
   D. role-playing simulations

12. Of the following, it is MOST likely to be proper for the agency head to allow the agency personnel officer to make final selection of appointees from certified eligible lists where there are 12.____
   A. *small* numbers of employees to be hired in newly-developed professional fields
   B. *large* numbers of persons to be hired for key managerial positions
   C. *large* numbers of persons to be hired in very routine occupations where the individual discretion of operating officials is not vital
   D. *small* numbers of persons to be hired in highly specialized professional occupations which are vital to the agency's operations

13. Of the following, an operating agency personnel office is LEAST likely to be able to exert strong influence or control within the operating agency by 13.____
   A. interpreting to the operating agency head what is intended by the directives and rules emanating from the central personnel agency
   B. establishing the key objectives of those line divisions of the operating agency employing large numbers of staff and operating under the management-by-objectives approach
   C. formulating and proposing to the agency head the internal policies and procedures on personnel matters required within the operating agency
   D. exercising certain discretionary authority in the application of the agency head's general personnel policies to actual specific situations

14. PERT is a recently developed system used PRIMARILY to 14.____
   A. evaluate the quality of applicants' background
   B. analyze and control the timing aspects of a major project
   C. control the total expenditure of agency funds within a monthly or quarterly time period
   D. analyze and control the differential effect on costs of purchasing different quantities

15. Assume that an operating agency has among its vacant positions two positions, each of which encompasses mixed duties. Both require appointees to have considerable education and experience, but these requirements are essential only for the more difficult duties of these positions. In the place of these positions, an administrator creates two new positions, one in which the higher duties are concentrated and the other with the lesser functions requiring only minimum preparation. 15.____
Of the following, it is generally MOST appropriate to characterize the administrator's action as a(n)
   A. *undesirable* example of deliberate downgrading of standards and requirements
   B. *undesirable* manipulation of the classification system for non-merit purposes
   C. *desirable* broadening of the definition of a class of positions
   D. *desirable* example of job redesign

16. Of the following, the LEAST important stumbling block to the development of personnel mobility among governmental jurisdictions is the 16.____
   A. limitations on lateral entry above junior levels in many jurisdictions
   B. continued collection of filing fees for civil service tests by many governmental jurisdictions
   C. absence of reciprocal exchange of retirement benefit eligibility between governments
   D. disparities in salary scales between governments

17. Of the following, the MAJOR disadvantage of a personnel system that features the *selection out* (forced retirement) of those who have been passed over a number of times for promotion is that such a system 17.____
   A. wastes manpower which is perfectly competent at one level but unable to rise above that level
   B. wastes funds by requiring review boards
   C. leads to excessive recruiting of newcomers from outside the system
   D. may not be utilized in *closed* career systems with low maximum age limits for entrance

18. Of the following, the fields in which operating agency personnel offices generally exercise the MOST stringent controls over first line supervisors in the agency are 18.____
   A. methods analysis and work simplification
   B. selection and position classification
   C. vestibule training and Gantt chart
   D. suggestion systems and staff development

19. Of the following, computers are normally MOST effective in handling 19.____
   A. large masses of data requiring simple processing
   B. small amounts of data requiring constantly changing complex processing
   C. data for which reported values are often subject to inaccuracies
   D. large amounts of data requiring continual programming and reprocessing

20. Contingency planning, which has long been used by the military and is assuming increasing importance in other organizations, may BEST be described as a process which utilizes 20.____
    A. alternative plans based on varying assumptions
    B. *crash programs* by organizations departmentalized along process lines
    C. plans which mandate substitution of equipment for manpower at predetermined operational levels
    D. plans that individually and accurately predict future events

21. In the management of inventory, two kinds of costs normally determine when to order and in what amounts. 21.____
The one of the following choices which includes BOTH of these kinds of costs is _____ costs and _____ costs.
    A. carrying; storage
    B. personnel; order
    C. computer; order
    D. personnel; computer

22. At top management levels, the one of the following which is generally the MOST important executive skill is skill in 22.____
    A. budgeting procedures
    B. a technical discipline
    C. controlling actions in accordance with previously approved plans
    D. seeing the organization as a whole

23. Of the following, the BEST way to facilitate the successful operation of a committee is to set guidelines establishing its 23.____
    A. budget exclusive of personnel costs
    B. location
    C. schedule of meetings or conferences
    D. scope of purpose

24. Executive training programs that single out particular managers and groom them for promotion create the so-called organizational *crown princes.* 24.____
Of the following, the MOST serious problem that arises in connection with this practice is that
    A. the managers chosen for promotion seldom turn out to be the best managers since the future potential of persons cannot be predicted
    B. not enough effort is made to remove organizational obstacles in the way of their development and achievement
    C. the resentment of the managers not selected for the program has an adverse effect on the motivation of those managers not selected
    D. performance appraisal and review are not carried out systematically enough

25. Of the following, the LEAST likely result of the use of the concept of job enlargement is that 25.____
    A. coordination will be simplified
    B. the individual's job will become less challenging
    C. worker satisfaction will increase
    D. fewer people will have to give attention to each piece of work

KEY (CORRECT ANSWERS)

1.	C	11.	A
2.	A	12.	C
3.	A	13.	B
4.	C	14.	B
5.	B	15.	D
6.	B	16.	B
7.	C	17.	A
8.	A	18.	B
9.	A	19.	A
10.	C	20.	A

21. A
22. D
23. D
24. C
25. B

TEST 2

DIRECTIONS: Each question or incomplete statement is followed by several suggested answers or completions. Select the one that BEST answers the question or completes the statement. *PRINT THE LETTER OF THE CORRECT ANSWER IN THE SPACE AT THE RIGHT.*

1. The one of the following which is MOST likely to be emphasized in the use of the brainstorming technique is the 1.____
   A. early consideration of cost factors of all ideas which may be suggested
   B. avoidance of impractical suggestions
   C. separation of the generation of ideas from their evaluation
   D. appraisal of suggestions concurrently with their initial presentation

2. Of the following, the BEST method for assessing managerial performance is generally to 2.____
   A. compare the manager's accomplishments against clear, specific, agreed-upon goals
   B. compare the manager's traits with those of his peers on a predetermined objective
   C. measure the manager's behavior against a listing of itemized personal traits
   D. measure the manager's success according to the enumeration of the *satisfaction* principle

3. As compared with recruitment from outside, selection from within the service must generally show GREATER concern for the 3.____
   A. prestige in which the public service as a whole is held by the public
   B. morale of the candidate group compromising the recruitment field
   C. cost of examining per candidate
   D. benefits of the use of standardized and validated tests

4. Performance budgeting focuses PRIMARY attention upon which one of the following? The 4.____
   A. things to be acquired, such as supplies and equipment
   B. general character and relative importance of the work to be done or the service to be rendered
   C. list of personnel to be employed, by specific title
   D. separation of employee performance evaluations from employee compensation

5. Of the following, the FIRST step in the installation and operation of a performance budgeting system generally should be the 5.____
   A. identification of program costs in relationship to the accounting system and operating structure
   B. identification of the specific end results of past programs in other jurisdictions

C. identification of work programs that are meaningful for management purposes
D. establishment of organizational structures each containing only one work program

6. Of the following, the MOST important purpose of a system of quarterly allotments of appropriated funds generally is to enable the 6.____
A. head of the judicial branch to determine the legality of agency requests for budget increases
B. operating agencies of government to upgrade the quality of their services without increasing costs
C. head of the executive branch to control the rate at which the operating agencies obligate and expend funds
D. operating agencies of government to avoid payment for services which have not been properly rendered by employees

7. In the preparation of the agency's budget, the agency's central budget office has two responsibilities: program review and management improvement. Which one of the following questions concerning an operating agency's program is MOST closely related to the agency budget officer's program review responsibility? 7.____
A. Can expenditures for supplies, materials, or equipment be reduced?
B. Will improved work methods contribute to a more effective program?
C. What is the relative importance of this program as compared to a higher level of program performance?
D. Will a realignment of responsibilities contribute to a higher level of program performance?

8. Of the following, the method of evaluating relative rates of return normally and generally thought to be MOST useful in evaluating government operations is _____ analysis. 8.____
A. cost-benefit
B. budget variance
C. investment capital
D. budget planning program

9. The one of the following assumptions that is LEAST likely to be made by a democratic or permissive type of leader is that 9.____
A. commitment to goals is seldom a result of monetary rewards alone
B. people can learn not only to accept, but also to seek, responsibility
C. the average person prefers security over advancement
D. creativity may be found in most segments of the population

10. In attempting to motivate subordinates, a manager should PRINCIPALLY be aware of the fact that 10.____
A. the psychological qualities of people, in general, are easily predictable
B. fear, as a traditional form of motivation, has lost much of its former power to motivate people in our modern industrial society
C. fear is still the most potent force in motivating the behavior of subordinates in the public service
D. the worker has very little control over the quality and quantity of his output

11. Assume that the following figures represent the number of work-unit that were produced during a week by each of sixteen employees in a division: 11.____

12	16	13	18
21	12	16	13
16	13	17	21
13	15	18	20

If all of the employees of the division who produced thirteen work-units during the week had instead produced fifteen work-units during that same week, then for that week the
   A. mean, median, and mode would all change
   B. mean and mode would change, but the median would remain the same
   C. mode and median would change, but the mean would remain the same
   D. mode, mean, and median would all still remain unchanged in value

12. An important law in motivation theory is called the *law of effect.* This law says that behavior which satisfies a person's needs tends to be repeated; behavior which does not satisfy a person's needs tends to be eliminated. 12.____
The one of the following which is the BEST interpretation of this law is that
   A. productivity depends on personality traits
   B. diversity of goals leads to instability and motivation
   C. the greater the satisfaction, the more likely it is that the behavior will be reinforced
   D. extrinsic satisfaction is more important than intrinsic reward

13. Of the following, the MOST acceptable reason an administrator can give for taking advice from other employees in the organization only when he asks for it is that he wants to 13.____
   A. encourage creativity and high morale
   B. keep dysfunctional pressures and inconsistent recommendations to a minimum
   C. show his superiors and peers who is in charge
   D. show his subordinates who is in charge

14. A complete picture of the communication channels in an organization can BEST be revealed by 14.____
   A. observing the planned paperwork system
   B. recording the highly intermittent patterns of communication
   C. plotting the entire flow of information over a period of time
   D. monitoring the *grapevine*

Questions 15-16.

DIRECTIONS: Questions 15 and 16 are to be answered SOLELY on the basis of the following passage.

Management by objectives (MBO) may be defined as the process by which the superior and the subordinate managers of an organization jointly define its common goals, define each individual's major areas of responsibility in terms of the results expected of him and use these measures as guides for operating the unit and assessing the contribution of each of its members.

The MBO approach requires that after organizational goals are established and communicated, targets must be set for each individual position which are congruent with organizational goals. Periodic performance reviews and a final review using the objectives set as criteria are also basic to this approach.

Recent studies have shown that MBO programs are influenced by attitudes and perceptions of the boss, the company, the reward-punishment system, and the program itself. In addition, the manner in which the MBO program is carried out can influence the success of the program. A study done in the late sixties indicates that the best results are obtained when the manager sets goals which deal with significant problem areas in the organizational unit, or with the subordinate's personal deficiencies. These goals must be clear with regard to what is expected of the subordinate. The frequency of feedback is also important in the success of a management-by-objectives program. Generally, the greater the amount of feedback, the more successful the MBO program.

15. According to the above passage, the expected output for individual employees should be determined 15.____
    A. after a number of reviews of work performance
    B. after common organizational goals are defined
    C. before common organizational goals are defined
    D. on the basis of an employee's personal qualities

16. According to the above passage, the management-by-objectives approach requires 16.____
    A. less feedback than other types of management programs
    B. little review of on-the-job performance after the initial setting of goals
    C. general conformance between individual goals and organizational goals
    D. the setting of goals which deal with minor problem area in the organization

Questions 17-19.

DIRECTIONS: Questions 17 through 19 are to be answered SOLELY on the basis of the following passage.

During the last decade, a great deal of interest has been generated around the phenomenon of organizational development, or the process of developing human resources through conscious organization effort. Organizational development (OD) stresses improving interpersonal relationships and organizational skills, such as communication, to a much greater degree than individual training ever did.

The kind of training that an organization should emphasize depends upon the present and future structure of the organization. If future organizations are to be unstable, shifting coalitions, then individual skills and abilities, particularly those emphasizing innovativeness, creativity, flexibility, and the latest technological knowledge, are crucial, and individual training is most appropriate.

But if there is to be little change in organizational structure, then the main thrust of training should be group-oriented or organizational development. This approach seems better designed for overcoming hierarchical barriers, for developing a degree of interpersonal relationships which make communication along the chain of command possible, and for retaining a modicum of innovation and/or flexibility.

17. According to the above passage, group-oriented training is MOST useful in 17.____
    A. developing a communications system that will facilitate understanding through the chain of command
    B. highly flexible and mobile organizations
    C. preventing the crossing of hierarchical barriers within an organization
    D. saving energy otherwise wasted on developing methods of dealing with rigid hierarchies

18. The one of the following conclusions which can be drawn MOST appropriately from the above passage is that 18.____
    A. behavioral research supports the use of organizational development training method rather than individualized training
    B. it is easier to provide individualized training in specific skills than to set up sensitivity training programs
    C. organizational development eliminates innovative or flexible activity
    D. the nature of an organization greatly influences which training methods will be most effective

19. According to the above passage, the one of the following which is LEAST important for large-scale organizations geared to rapid and abrupt change is 19.____
    A. current technological information
    B. development of a high degree of interpersonal relationships
    C. development of individual skills and abilities
    D. emphasis on creativity

Questions 20-25.

DIRECTIONS: Each of Questions 20 through 25 consist of a statement which contains one word that is incorrectly used because it is not in keeping with the meaning that the quotation is evidently intended to convey. Determine which word is INCORRECTLY used. Select from the choices lettered A, B, C, and D the word which, when substituted for the incorrectly used word, would BEST help to convey the meaning of the statement.

20. One of the considerations likely to affect the currency of classification, particularly in professional and managerial occupations, is the impact of the incumbent's capacities on the job. Some work is highly susceptible to change as the result of the special talents or interests of the classifier. Organization should never be so rigid as not to capitalize on the innovative or unusual proclivities of its key employees. While a machine operator may not be able, even subtly, to change the character or level of his job, the design engineer, the attorney, or the organization and methods analyst might readily do so. Reliance on his judgment and the scope of his assignments may both grow as the result of his skill, insight, and capacity. 20.____
A. unlikely B. incumbent C. directly D. scope

21. The supply of services by the state is not governed by market price. The aim is to supply such services to all who need them and to treat all consumers equally. This objective especially compels the civil servant to maintain a role f strict impartiality, based on the principle of equality of individual citizens vis-à-vis their government. However, there is a clear difference between being neutral and impartial. If the requirement is construed to mean that all civil servants should be political eunuchs, devoid of the drive and motivation essential to dynamic administration, then the concept of impartiality is being seriously utilized. Modern governments should not be stopped from demanding that their hirelings have not only the technical but the emotional qualifications necessary for whole-hearted effort. 21.____
A. determined B. rule C. stable D. misapplied

22. The manager was barely listening. Recently, at the divisional level, several new fronts of troubles had erupted, including a requirement to increase production yet hold down operating costs and somehow raise quality standards. Though the three objectives were basically obsolete, top departmental management was insisting on the simultaneous attainment of them, an insistence not helping the manager's ulcer, an old enemy within. Thus, the manager could not find time for interest in individuals—only in statistics which regiment of individuals, like unconsidered Army privates, added up to. 22.____
A. quantity B. battalion C. incompatible D. quiet

23. When a large volume of data flows directly between operators and first-line supervisors, senior executives tend to be out of the mainstream of work. Summary reports can increase their remoteness. An executive needs to know the volume, quality, and cost of completed work, and exceptional problems. In addition, he may desire information on key operating conditions. Summary reports on these matters are, therefore, essential features of a communications network and make delegation without loss of control possible. 23.____
A. unimportant B. quantity C. offset D. incomplete

24. Of major significance in management is harmony between the overall objectives of the organization and the managerial objectives within that organization. In addition, harmony among goals of managers is impossible; they should not be at cross-purposes. Each manager's goal should supplement and assist the goals of his colleagues. Likewise, the objectives of individuals or non-management members should be harmonized with those of the manager. When this is accomplished, genuine teamwork is the result, and human relations are aided materially. The integration of managers' and individuals' goals aids in achieving greater work satisfaction at all levels. 24.____
    A. competition B. dominate C. incremental D. vital

25. Change constantly challenges the manager. Some of this change is evolutionary, some revolutionary, some recognizable, some non-recognizable. Both forces within an enterprise and forces outside the enterprise cause managers to act and react in initiating changes in their immediate working environment. Change invalidates existing operations. Goals are not being accomplished in the best manner, problems develop, and frequently because of the lack of time, only patched-up solutions are followed. The result is that the mode of management is profound in nature and temporary in effectiveness. A complete overhaul of managerial operations should take place. It appears quite likely that we are just beginning to see the real effects of change in our society; the pace probably will accelerate in ways that few really understand or know how to handle. 25.____
    A. confirms B. decline C. instituting D. superficial

KEY (CORRECT ANSWERS)

1.	C	11.	B
2.	A	12.	C
3.	B	13.	B
4.	B	14.	C
5.	C	15.	B
6.	C	16.	C
7.	C	17.	A
8.	A	18.	D
9.	C	19.	B
10.	B	20.	B

21.	D
22.	C
23.	C
24.	D
25.	D

EXAMINATION SECTION

TEST 1

DIRECTIONS: Each question or incomplete statement is followed by several suggested answers or completions. Select the one that BEST answers the question or completes the statement. *PRINT THE LETTER OF THE CORRECT ANSWER IN THE SPACE AT THE RIGHT.*

1. The one of the following which BEST characterizes an agency in which delegation of authority is practiced on an organization-wide level is that the agency is 1.____
   A. autocratic
   B. authoritarian
   C. centralized
   D. decentralized

2. The concept of the *chain of command* is MOST similar to which one of the following concepts? 2.____
   A. Span of control
   B. Matrix or task-force organization
   C. Scalar principle
   D. Functional departmentation

3. The one of the following techniques which is NOT conducive to the establishment of an effective working relationship between employees and supervisors is 3.____
   A. periodic discussion of job performance with employees
   B. listening to employees when they discuss their job difficulties
   C. observation of employees on the job, in both individual and group situations, in order to help them with job performance
   D. treating all employees the same with respect to job performance and individual behavior

4. Which of the following is a valid, commonly-raised objection to the establishment of work standards for office clerical workers? 4.____
   A. Routine clerical work is not subject to accurate measurement.
   B. Clerical work standards can only lower employee morale by creating undue pressure to produce work rapidly.
   C. Work standards are not effective tools for planning, scheduling, and routing clerical work.
   D. Some phases of many clerical jobs, such as telephone answering or information gathering, cannot be readily or accurately measured.

5. Of the following, the feature which is LEAST characteristic of almost all successful staff relationships with line managers is that the staff employee 5.____
   A. is primarily a representative of his supervisor
   B. receives a salary at least equal to the average salary of his supervisor's direct line subordinates
   C. relies largely on persuasion to get his ideas put into effect
   D. is prepared to submerge his own personality and his own desire for recognition and see others often receive more recognition than he receives

6. The one of the following systems which has, as its principal objective, the storage of items in files so that they may be readily found when needed is called 6.____
   A. information retrieval
   B. simulation
   C. critical path
   D. PERT

7. A detailed description of the steps to be taken in order to accomplish a job is MOST appropriately called a 7.____
   A. policy
   B. rule
   C. procedure
   D. principle

8. In choosing the best place in the executive hierarchy to which to assign the task of making a certain type of decision, which one of the following should normally be LEAST important? 8.____
   A. Who knows the facts on which the decision will be based, or who can obtain them most readily?
   B. Who has the most adequate supply of current forms on which the decision is normally recorded?
   C. Who has the capacity to make sound decisions?
   D. How significant is the decision?

9. Of the following, the action which is LEAST likely to be either expressed or implied every time a manager delegates work to a subordinate is that the manager 9.____
   A. creates a need for a new class of positions
   B. indicates what work the subordinate is to do
   C. grants the subordinate some authority
   D. creates an obligation for the subordinate who accepts the work to try to complete it

10. Of the following, the LEAST appropriate use of organizational charts is to 10.____
   A. depict standard operating procedures
   B. indicate lines of responsibility
   C. indicate the relative level of key positions
   D. portray organizations graphically

11. The one of the following considerations which is generally LEAST important in deciding whether to automate a management operation by using a computer is whether the computer 11.____
   A. possesses a suitable array of programmed actions that might be taken
   B. can draw upon available data for information as to which alternative is best
   C. is already familiar to the staff of the organization
   D. can issue findings in a way that will facilitate the decision-making process

12. In evaluating a proposal to establish a library in your agency, it is generally considered LEAST necessary to determine 12.____
    A. the average time staff members spend on preparatory research when assigned to projects
    B. how often junior professional and technical staff members are sent out to *look something up* in a local library
    C. how much time and money agency executives devote to telephoning around the country seeking information before making decisions
    D. the quality of the research done by executives and scientists in the agency

13. In determining the number and type of tasks that should be combined into a single job, the one of the following which is normally the LEAST useful factor to consider is the 13.____
    A. benefit of functional specialization
    B. benefit of tall pyramid organization structures in increasing decentralization
    C. need for coordination of tasks with each other
    D. effect of the tasks assigned on the morale of the employee

14. Of the following, the one which is LEAST likely to be an objective of systems and procedures analysis is to 14.____
    A. eliminate as many unessential forms and records as feasible
    B. simplify forms in content and method of preparation
    C. mechanize repetitive, routine tasks
    D. expand as many of the forms as possible

15. A specific managerial function encompasses all of the following: The establishment of an intentional structure of roles through determination and enumeration of the activities required to achieve the goals of an enterprise and each part of it, the grouping of these activities, the assignment of such groups of activities to a manager, the delegation of authority to carry them out, and provision for coordination of authority and informational relationships horizontally and vertically in the organization structure. 15.____
    Of the following, the MOST appropriate term for this entire managerial function is
    A. organizing B. directing C. controlling D. staffing

16. The optimum number of subordinates that a supervisor can supervise effectively generally tends to vary INVERSELY with the 16.____
    A. percentage of the supervisor's time devoted to supervision rather than operations
    B. repetition of activities
    C. degree of centralization of decision-making within the supervisor's unit
    D. ability of subordinates

17. Under certain circumstances, a top manager may desire to strengthen the position of his staff people by granting them concurring authority, so that no action may be taken in a functional area by subordinate line officials until a designated staff employee agrees to the action. For example, office manages may have to get the approval of the agency personnel officer before hiring a new employee. 17.____
This approach is likely to be MOST valid under which one of the following conditions?
    A. The top manager refrains from indicating the grounds on which the staff employee may grant or withhold his approval of line proposals.
    B. The point of view represented by the staff employee is particularly important, and the possible delay in action will not be serious.
    C. It is more important to fix specific accountability for failure to take appropriate action than for wrong actions taken.
    D. The top manager gives speed priority over prudence.

18. The inclusion of the reason why a superior in his written orders to his subordinates normally is MOST likely to 18.____
    A. encourage belief by the subordinates in the meaning and intent of the order
    B. be a waste of valuable time for both superior and subordinates
    C. be useful principally where the superior has no power to enforce the order
    D. discourage effective two-way communication between superior and subordinates

19. The one of the following which is generally LEAST justification for an administrator's search for alternative methods of attaining a given objective of the unit he heads is that such search 19.____
    A. always turns up a better method of attaining objectives than that currently in use
    B. helps to make certain that the best method has a chance to be found and evaluated
    C. helps to insure that his peers realize that the existing method of attaining the objective is not the best
    D. is a good way to train the unit's staff in the organization's operational procedures

20. *Managing-by-Objectives* tends to place PRINCIPAL emphasis upon which of the following? 20.____
    A. Use of primarily qualitative goals at all management levels
    B. Use of trait-appraisal systems based upon personality factors
    C. Use of primarily qualitative goals at lower management levels as contrasted with primarily quantitative goals at higher management levels
    D. Goals which are clear and verifiable

21. Which one of the following BEST identifies the two most important considerations which generally should determine the degree of management decentralization desirable in a given situation? The 21.____
    A. age of the subordinate executives to whom decisions may be delegated and the number of courses in management that they have completed
    B. number of skills and the competence possessed by subordinate executives and the distribution of the necessary information to the points of decision
    C. ratio of the salary of the superior executives to the salary of the subordinate executives and the number of titles on the executive staff
    D. number of titles in the executive staff and the distribution of information to those various titles

22. Which one of the following is generally LEAST likely to occur at mid-level management as a result of installing an electronic data processing system? 22.____
    A. The time that managers will be required to spend on the controlling function will increase.
    B. The number of contacts that managers will have with subordinates will increase.
    C. Additional time will be needed to train people for managerial positions.
    D. There will be an increase in the volume of information presented to managers for analysis.

23. The concept that the major source of managerial authority is derived from the subordinate's acceptance of the manager's power is MOST closely identified with 23.____
    A. Luther Gulick
    B. John D. Mooney
    C. Frederick W. Taylor
    D. Chester I. Barnard

24. The one of the following which is generally the principal objection to a pure *functional organization*, as compared with a pure *line organization*, is that 24.____
    A. there is a tendency to overload intermediate and supervisory management at each succeeding level of organization with wide and varied duties
    B. authority flows in an unbroken line from top management to the worker
    C. workers must often report to two or more supervisors
    D. there is a lack of specialization at the supervisory level

25. The appraisal of subordinates and their performance is an integral part of the supervisor's job. There is wide agreement that several basic principles must be taken into account by supervisors involved in the appraisal process in order to perform this function correctly. 25.____
    The one of the following statements which LEAST represents a basic principle of the appraisal process is:
    Appraisal(s)
    A. should be based more on performance of definite tasks than on personality considerations
    B. of long-range potential should rely most heavily on subjective judgment of that potential

C. involves the use of value judgments by the supervisor and does, therefore, require reference to pre-established standards
D. should aim at emphasizing subordinates' strengths rather than weaknesses

26. Of the following, the INITIAL step in the decision-making procedure normally is 26.____
A. evaluation of alternatives
B. implementing the chosen course of action
C. listing potential solutions
D. diagnosis and problem definition

27. Management textbooks are LEAST likely to define coordination as 27.____
A. a concern for harmonious and unified action directed toward a common objective
B. the essence of management, since the basic purpose of management is the achievement of harmony of individual effort toward the accomplishment of group goals
C. the orderly arrangement of group effort to provide unity of action in pursuit of common purpose
D. the transmittal of messages from senders to receivers, involving acts of persuasion of regulation, or simply the rendering of information

28. A number of important assumptions underlie the modern human relations approach to management and administration. 28.____
The one of the following which is NOT an assumption integral to the human relations school of thought is that
A. employee participation is essential to higher productivity
B. employees are motivated solely by monetary factors
C. teamwork is indispensable for organization growth and survival
D. free-flow communications must be established and maintained for organizational effectiveness

29. Of the following, the MAIN purpose of systematic manpower planning is to 29.____
A. analyze the levels of skill needed by each worker
B. analyze causes of current vacancies, such as resignations, discharges, retirements, transfers, or promotions
C. save money by eliminating useless jobs
D. provide for the continuous and proper staffing of the workforce

30. A Planning-Programming-Budget System (PPBS) is PRIMARILY intended to do which of the following? 30.____
A. Improve control through a budgeting-by-line-item system
B. Plan and program budgets by objective rather than by function
C. Raise money for social welfare programs
D. Reduce budgets by planning and programming unspent funds

KEY (CORRECT ANSWERS)

1.	D	11.	C	21.	B
2.	C	12.	D	22.	A
3.	D	13.	B	23.	D
4.	D	14.	D	24.	C
5.	B	15.	A	25.	B
6.	A	16.	C	26.	D
7.	C	17.	B	27.	D
8.	B	18.	A	28.	B
9.	A	19.	B	29.	D
10.	A	20.	D	30.	B

TEST 2

DIRECTIONS: Each question or incomplete statement is followed by several suggested answers or completions. Select the one that BEST answers the question or completes the statement. *PRINT THE LETTER OF THE CORRECT ANSWER IN THE SPACE AT THE RIGHT.*

1. An administrative office is designed so that several administrative associates can log on to Microsoft Outlook and use an e-mail inbox that syncs in real time. Each associate can also send jobs to a central office printer. This is an example of 1.____
   A. network connectivity B. cloud connectivity
   C. office integration D. employee training

2. In the planning of office space for the various bureaus and divisions of an agency, the one of the following arrangements which is generally considered to be MOST desirable in a conventional layout is to 2.____
   A. locate offices where employees do close and tedious work, such as accounting, and also offices of high-level executives away from windows so that distractions will be minimal
   B. locate *housekeeping* offices such as data processing and the mailroom very close to the high executive offices to increase convenience for the executives
   C. locate departments so that the work flow proceeds in an uninterrupted manner
   D. centralize the executive suite for maximum availability and public exposure

3. Generally, the one of the following that is LEAST likely to be an essential step in a records retention plan is 3.____
   A. storing inactive records
   B. checking for accuracy of all records to be retained
   C. classification of all records
   D. making an inventory of all agency records

4. The PRINCIPAL asset of an office layout diagram, as contrasted with the more abstract organization charts and flowcharts, is that an office layout diagram is 4.____
   A. more readily adaptable to strictly conceptual studies
   B. pictorial and therefore easier to understand
   C. suitable for showing both manual and machine processing operations, whereas organization charts and flowcharts may only be used for manual processing operations
   D. better suited for summarizing the number of work units produced at each step

5. One of the assistants whom you supervise displays apparent familiarity toward a businessman who deals with your agency. This assistant spends more time with this person than the nature of his business would warrant, and you have observed that they are occasionally seen leaving the office together for lunch. In several instances, when this businessman comes into the office and this assistant is not at his desk, the businessman will not deal with any other staff member but will, instead, leave the office and return later when that particular employee is available. 5.____
Of the following courses of action, the FIRST one you should take is to
   A. audit the agency's books and records pertaining to this businessman
   B. rebuke the assistant for unprofessional conduct at the next staff meeting and warn him of disciplinary action if the practice is not discontinued forthwith
   C. advise your agency head of the action by the businessman and the assistant that has been described in the above paragraph
   D. reassign the assistant to duties that will not bring him into contact with any businessman

6. The one of the following factors which generally is the BEST justification for keeping higher inventories of supplies and equipment is an expected 6.____
   A. decline in demand
   B. price increase
   C. decline in prices
   D. increase in interest charges and storage costs

7. Statistical sampling is often used in administrative operations PRIMARILY because it enables 7.____
   A. administrators to determine the characteristics of appointed or elected officials
   B. decisions to be made based on mathematical and scientific fact
   C. courses of action to be determined by scientifically-based computer programs
   D. useful predictions to be made from relatively small samples

8. According to United States Department of Labor figures, the PRINCIPAL source of disabling injuries to office workers is 8.____
   A. flying objects and falling objects
   B. striking against equipment
   C. falls and slips
   D. handling materials

9. To expedite the processing of applications issued by your agency, you ask your assistant to design a form that will be used by your typists. After several discussions, he presents you with a draft that requires the typist to use 23 tabular-stop positions. 9.____
Such a form would PROBABLY be considered
   A. *undesirable*; typists would now have to soft-roll the platen to make the typing fall on the lines
   B. *desirable*; the fill-in operation by typists would be speeded up

C. *undesirable*; proper vertical alignment of data would be made difficult by the number of tabular-stop positions required
D. *desirable*; it would force the typists to utilize the tabular-stop device

Question 10.

DIRECTIONS: Following are five general instructions to file clerks which might appear in the proposed filing manual for an agency.

I. Follow instructions generally; if you have a suggestion for improvement in the filing methods, install it after notifying the file supervisor who will duly authorize a change in the manual.
II. You may discuss the contents of files with fellow employees or outsiders, but do NOT give papers from the file to any person whose duties have no relation to the material requested.
III. All special instructions must be given by the file supervisor. Any problems that arise outside the regular routine of filing must be decided by the file supervisor, not by a fellow clerk.
IV. You will not be held responsible for your own errors; thus, refrain from asking other workers for instructions. No one is more interested in helping you in your training than your file supervisor.
V. Speed is the first essential in filing; make it your primary consideration—quick finding of filed material is the real test of your efficiency.

10. Which of the choices listed below BEST identifies those of the above statements that should or should not be followed by agencies in the functioning of their filing sections? 10.____
Instruction(s) _____ should be followed; instructions _____ should not be followed.
A. I, II, III; IV, V
B. III; I, II, IV, V
C. II, IV; I, III, V
D. I, III; II, IV, V

11. Listed below are five steps in the process of staffing: 11.____
I. Authorization for staffing
II. Manpower planning
III. Development of applicant sources
IV. Evaluation of applicants
V. Employment decisions and offers
The one of the following sequences which is generally the MOST logical arrangement of the above steps is:
A. I, II, III, IV, V
B. II, I, III, IV, V
C. III, I, II, IV, V
D. II, III, I, IV, V

12. Job enrichment is LEAST likely to lead to 12.____
A. fewer employee grievances
B. increased employee productivity
C. people acting as adjuncts of increased automation
D. increased employee morale

13. Of the following, programmed instruction would usually be MOST effective in teaching 13.____
   A. principles of decision-making
   B. technical skills and knowledge
   C. good judgment
   D. executive management ability

14. Assume that a group has been working effectively with a contributing nonconformist in its midst. 14.____
The BEST of the following reasons for the group to retain the nonconformist generally is that
   A. nonconformists stimulate groups to think
   B. he may be their boss some day
   C. nonconformists usually are fun to work with
   D. another nonconformist will usurp his role

15. The *grievance-arbitration* process involves systematic union-management deliberation regarding a complaint that work- or contract-related. 15.____
An outcome that does NOT result from this process is
   A. a communications channel from the rank-and-file workers to higher management is developed or improved
   B. the contract is immediately changed to provide justice for both parties
   C. both labor and management identify those parts of the contract that need to be clarified and modified in subsequent negotiations
   D. the language of the agreement is informally translated into understandable terms for the parties bound by it

16. In government, job evaluation is the process of determining the relative worth of the various jobs in an organization so that differential wages can be paid. 16.____
Job evaluation is based on several basic assumptions.
Of the assumptions listed below, the MOST questionable is that
   A. the cash payments in government should be substantially higher than those in local private industry
   B. it is logical to pay the most for jobs that contribute most to the organization
   C. people feel more fairly treated if wages are based on the relative worth of their jobs
   D. the best way to achieve the goals of the enterprise is to maintain a wage structure based on job worth

17. Of the following, the training method that normally provides the instructor with the LEAST *feedback* from the trainees is 17.____
   A. the lecture method
   B. the conference method
   C. simulation or gaming techniques
   D. seminar instruction

18. Insufficient and inappropriate delegation of work assignments is MOST often the fault of 18.____
   A. subordinates who are unwilling to accept responsibility for their own mistakes
   B. a paternal attitude on the part of management

C. the immediate supervisor
D. subordinates who are too willing to take on extra responsibility

19. As contrasted with expense budgets, capital budgets are MORE likely to 19.____
A. be used for construction of physical facilities
B. be designed for a shorter time period
C. include personal service expenditures
D. include fringe benefits

20. During the first quarter of a year, a division's production rate was 1.26 man-hours per work unit produced. For the second quarter of that year, all other factors (e.g., size of staff, character of work unit, etc.) remained constant, except that the manner of reporting production rate was changed to work units per man-hour instead of man-hours per work unit. During that second quarter, the unit's production rate was .89 work units per man-hour. 20.____
On the basis of the above information, it would be MOST NEARLY CORRECT to conclude that the division's production rate during the second quarter was approximately _____ than during the first quarter.
A. 30% lower B. 10% lower C. 10% higher D. 30% higher

Questions 21-22.

DIRECTIONS: Questions 21 and 22 are to be answered on the basis of the following information.

The five bureaus within a department sent the following budget requests to the department head:

Bureau A: $10 million
Bureau B: $12 million
Bureau C: $18 million
Bureau D: $6 million
Bureau E: $4 million

After reviewing all of these requests, the department head decided to reduce these requests so that they would total only $40 million. He considered the following two options to accomplish this:

Option I: Reduce the requests of Bureaus A, B, and D by an equal dollar amount. Reduce the dollar amount request of Bureau C by 2½ times the dollar amount that he reduces the request of Bureau B. Reduce the dollar amount request of Bureau E by ½ of the dollar amount that he reduces the request of Bureau B.

Option II: First, reduce the dollar amount request of all five bureaus by 15%. Then, the remaining reduction required by the entire department would be achieved by further reducing the resulting budget requests of Bureaus B and C by an equal dollar amount each.

21. Under Option I, the dollar amount request for Bureau E, after reduction by the department head, would be MOST NEARLY _____ millions. 21._____
   A. $1²/₃ B. $2¹/₃ C. $3¹/₆ D. $3½

22. Under Option II, the dollar amount of the request of Bureau B, after both reductions were made by the department head, would be MOST NEARLY _____ millions. 22._____
   A. $8 B. $9 C. $10 D. $11

23. The Summary of finding of a long management report intended for typical manager should generally appear _____ the report. 23._____
   A. at the very beginning of
   B. at the end of the report
   C. throughout
   D. in the middle of

24. Of the following, the BIGGEST disadvantage in allowing a free flow of communications in an agency is that such a free flow 24._____
   A. decreases creativity
   B. increases the use of the *grapevine*
   C. lengthens the chain of command
   D. reduces the executive's power to direct the flow of information

25. A downward flow of authority in an organization is one example of _____ communications. 25._____
   A. horizontal B. informal C. circular D. vertical

26. Workers who belong to a cohesive group are generally thought to 26._____
   A. have more job-related anxieties than those who do not
   B. be less well-adjusted than those who do not
   C. derive little satisfaction from the group
   D. Conform to group norms more closely than those in noncohesive groups

27. The one of the following which BEST exemplifies negative motivation is 27._____
   A. a feeling on the part of the worker that the work is significant
   B. monetary rewards offered the worker for high levels of output
   C. reducing or withholding the worker's incentive rewards when performance is mediocre
   D. nonmonetary rewards given the worker, such as publicizing a good suggestion

28. Of the following, the one that would be MOST likely to block effective communication is 28._____
   A. concentration only on the issues at hand
   B. lack of interest or commitment
   C. use of written reports
   D. use of charts and graphs

29. Many functions formerly centralized in a department of personnel have been decentralized, in whole or in part, to operating agencies. 29.____
The one of the following personnel functions which has been LEAST decentralized is
    A. positive evaluation
    B. investigation of non-competitive employees
    C. investigation of competitive employees
    D. jurisdictional classification

30. In making a position analysis for a duties classification, the one of the following factors which MUST be considered is the _____ the incumbent. 30.____
    A. capabilities of
    B. qualifications of
    C. efficiency attained by
    D. responsibility assigned to

KEY (CORRECT ANSWERS)

1.	A	11.	B	21.	C
2.	C	12.	C	22.	B
3.	B	13.	B	23.	A
4.	B	14.	A	24.	D
5.	C	15.	B	25.	D
6.	B	16.	A	26.	D
7.	D	17.	A	27.	C
8.	C	18.	C	28.	B
9.	C	19.	A	29.	D
10.	B	20.	C	30.	D

EXAMINATION SECTION
TEST 1

DIRECTIONS: Each question or incomplete statement is followed by several suggested answers or completions. Select the one that BEST answers the question or completes the statement. *PRINT THE LETTER OF THE CORRECT ANSWER IN THE SPACE AT THE RIGHT.*

1. Of the following factors, which one is LEAST important in determining the size of staff needed in conducting an organization survey?
   The

   A. effectiveness of the personnel in supplying data for the study
   B. extent of report writing anticipated
   C. number of field locations and headquarters staff units to be covered
   D. number of individuals to be interviewed as part of fact finding

2. In planning a systems survey, which one of the following is MOST important in carrying out an effective survey after the purpose and scope of the survey has been determined? The

   A. format of the survey report
   B. methods and techniques to be employed
   C. personality problems which may materialize
   D. exact starting and completion dates

3. Which of the following is the BEST way of organizing a final report?

   A. Begin and end the report with a summary of conclusions showing how conclusions were changed as a result of findings and recommendations
   B. Begin the report with an overall summary and then place findings and recommendations in several sections
   C. Intertwine findings and conclusions in such a manner as to make the report readable and interesting
   D. Place the findings and recommendations in separate sections avoiding conclusions to the maximum extent possible

4. Which of the following disadvantages is the MOST serious in making reports verbally rather than in writing?

   A. An effective analyst may not be a good public speaker.
   B. Verbal reports are conveniently forgotten.
   C. It may not generate actions and follow-through by recipients.
   D. There is a lack of permanent record to which one may later refer.

5. Following a management survey, which of the following represents the MOST serious pitfall which may be made in recommending improvements?

   A. Failure to convince people of the benefits to be derived from the recommendations
   B. Failure to freely discuss recommendations with those who must live with them
   C. Tendency of the survey team to put their own personalities into the report
   D. Tendency to deal in personalities instead of dealing with objectives and sound management practices

6. A working outline for management analysts should include all of the following EXCEPT

   A. a chronological outline of the work steps
   B. a determination of background information needed
   C. the distribution of outline to key staff and line personnel
   D. preliminary conclusions

7. Which one of the following areas is the MOST critical for an analyst during the fact-finding stage of a study?

   A. Accuracy of data appearing in reports
   B. Attitude of those being interviewed by the analyst
   C. Observations and tentative conclusions reached by the analyst
   D. Suggestions and recommendations of interviewees

8. Creating an organization embraces all of the following areas of management EXCEPT

   A. clarification of objectives
   B. determining the number of people required to man the organization
   C. establishing operating budgets to make the plan effective
   D. proper structuring of all key positions

9. In an organization, the MAJOR barrier to accepting change is the

   A. assumption by management that everyone will willingly accept change
   B. failure by management to present proposed changes in a proper fashion
   C. lack of adaptive abilities on the part of employees
   D. lack of understanding on the part of employees of sound management principles

10. A supervisor who wishes to attain established objectives should concentrate on

    A. determining whether management is operating at maximum effectiveness
    B. making suggestions for improving the organization
    C. planning work assignments
    D. securing salary increases for needy employees

11. A usually competent employee complains that he does not understand the procedures to be followed in performing a certain task although the supervisor has explained them twice and has demonstrated them.
    Of the following, the BEST course of action for the supervisor to take is to

    A. ask the employee whether he has any problems which are bothering him
    B. assign someone else to the job
    C. explain the procedures again and demonstrate at the same time
    D. have the employee perform the job while he watches and gives additional instructions

12. GENERALLY, in order to be completely qualified as a supervisor, a person

    A. should be able to perform exceptionally well at least one of the jobs he supervises and have some knowledge of the others
    B. must have an intimate working knowledge of all facets of the jobs which he supervises
    C. should know the basic principles and procedures of the jobs he supervises
    D. need know little or nothing of the jobs which he supervises as long as he knows the principles of supervision

13. Which of the following contributes MOST to the problem of waste and inefficiency in offices?

    A. Cost control is a budget function primarily.
    B. Most organizations do not have soundly conceived budgets.
    C. Procedures improvement staffs have not as yet gained acceptance among white-collar workers.
    D. Supervisors generally are uninterested in making improvements.

14. Which of the following contributes MOST to the great number of duplicate reports and double-checking procedures frequently found in offices?
    The

    A. desire for protection
    B. desire to improve problem solving
    C. intent to *manage by exception*
    D. need for budget data

15. Which one of the following BEST identifies the narrow technician as compared with the broad-gauged analyst?
    He

    A. analyzes the activities of an agency
    B. attempts to form sound relationships with departmental personnel
    C. focuses attention on forms design and appearance
    D. follows work flow from one bureau to another by charting operational steps

16. The percentage of budget funds allocated to fixed overhead costs can be MOST effectively reduced by

    A. a soundly conceived *promotion from within* policy
    B. increasing the amount of work performed
    C. relocating to areas closer to the center of cities
    D. tightening the *fixed cost* portion of the budget

17. The term *span of control* USUALLY refers to

    A. individuals reporting to a common supervisor
    B. individuals with whom one individual has contact in the course of performing his assigned duties
    C. levels of supervision in an organization
    D. percentage of time in an organization devoted to supervisory duties

18. For an analyst, which of the following is generally LEAST important in conducting a management survey?

    A. Ability of employees to understand goals of the survey
    B. Attitude of supervisors of employees
    C. Availability of employees for interviews
    D. Cooperation of employees

19. Of the following, morale in an agency is generally MOST significantly affected by

    A. agency policies and procedures
    B. agency recognition of executives supporting agency goals
    C. the extent to which an agency meets its announced goals
    D. the number of management surveys conducted in an agency

20. Which of the following BEST describes the principle of *management by exception?*

    A. Allocating executive time and effort in direct relation to the dollar values of the budget
    B. Decentralizing management and dealing primarily with problem areas
    C. Measuring only direct costs
    D. Setting goals and objectives and managing only these

21. A WEAKNESS of many budgetary systems today is that they

    A. are subjectively determined by those most directly involved
    B. focus on management weakness rather than management strength
    C. only show variable costs
    D. show in detail why losses are occurring

22. Standards on which budgets are developed should be based PRIMARILY on

    A. a general consensus
    B. agency wishes
    C. analytical studies
    D. historical performance

23. The income, cost, and expense goals making up a budget are aimed at achieving a predetermined objective but do not necessarily measure the lowest possible costs. This is PRIMARILY so because

    A. budget committees are accounting-oriented and are not sympathetic with the supervisor's personnel problems
    B. budget committees fail to recognize the difference between direct and indirect costs
    C. the level of expenditures provided for in a budget by budget committees is frequently an arbitrary rather than a scientifically determined amount
    D. budget committees spend considerable time evaluating data to the point that the material gathered is not representative or current

24. Linear programming has all of the following characteristics EXCEPT: It

    A. is concerned with an optimum position in relation to some objective
    B. involves the selection among alternatives or the appropriate combination of alternatives
    C. not only requires that variables be qualitative but also rests on the assumption that the relations among the variables are minimized
    D. takes into account constraints or limits within which the decision is to be reached

25. In the PERT planning system, the time in which a non-critical task can slip schedule without holding up a project is USUALLY called

    A. constraint
    B. duration time
    C. dead time
    D. float or slack

26. The Produc-trol board and Schedugraphs are commercial variations of the ______ chart.

    A. flow
    B. Gantt
    C. layout
    D. multiple activity

27. The item which cannot be analyzed by such schematic techniques as the frequency polygon and the histogram is the

    A. age of accounts receivable
    B. morale and cohesiveness of work groups
    C. number of accidents in a plant
    D. wage pattern

28. An essential employee benefit of work measurement which FREQUENTLY is the key to the successful implementation of such a program is

    A. equitable work distribution
    B. facilitation of the development of budgets
    C. measurement and control of office productivity
    D. prevention of unfair work distribution

29. An organizational arrangement whereby different employees perform different work steps upon the same work items at the same time is called the ______ method.

    A. functional
    B. homogenous
    C. parallel or linear arrangement
    D. unit assembly

30. Frequently, opposition to a management survey stems from an executive's feeling that he might be considered responsible for the unsatisfactory conditions that the project is aimed at correcting.
    To overcome this type of opposition, the analyst should GENERALLY

    A. avoid the issue altogether
    B. face the situation *head on* and, if the executive is responsible, tell him so
    C. offer a reasonable explanation for those conditions early enough in the discussion to forestall any implication of criticism
    D. place the blame for the unsatisfactory conditions at the lowest level in the organization to avoid incriminating the boss

31. Which of the following situations is LEAST likely to require a management survey?

    A. Changes in policy
    B. Management requests for additional manpower
    C. Legislation mandating changes in operating procedures
    D. Significantly lower costs than anticipated

32. The efficiency of a procedure is often influenced by the practices or performance of departments that play no direct part in carrying it out.
In view of this, the analyst must

    A. disregard the practices or performance of departments that play no direct part in the procedure
    B. do the very best job within the department studied to compensate for the outside problems
    C. ask for assistance in solving the problems created by this situation
    D. study and evaluate the external factors to the extent that they bear on the problem

33. Which one of the following is NOT a key step in staff delegation and development?

    A. Evaluation of the completed job
    B. Preparation of a subordinate to accept additional duties
    C. Review of daily progress
    D. Selection of a suitable job to be delegated

34. Which one of the following is NOT an essential characteristic of effective delegation?

    A. In delegating, the supervisor is no longer responsible.
    B. The individual to whom authority is delegated must be accountable for fulfillment of the task.
    C. The individual to whom authority is delegated must clearly understand this authority
    D. The individual to whom authority is delegated must get honest recognition for a job well done.

35. Whenever a manager must determine how long an operation should take, he is involved with the problem of setting a time standard.
To PROPERLY set time standards, the manager must distinguish between

    A. estimation processes and evaluation processes
    B. performance of the slowest employee and performance of the fastest employee
    C. stop watch study and work sampling
    D. synthetic and arbitrary systems

36. Assuming a report is needed, which approach USUALLY facilitates implementation?
A

    A. draft report submitted to key people for review, discussion, modification, and then resubmission in final form
    B. report in final form which sets forth alternate recommended solutions
    C. report which sets forth the problems and the recommended solution in conformance with the desires of those most directly involved
    D. visual presentation with minimal report writing

37. Of the following elements, which is the LEAST important in writing a survey report? A

    A. definite course of action to be followed
    B. listing of benefits to be gained through implementation
    C. review of opinions as differentiated from facts
    D. summary of conclusions

38. Physical appearance and accuracy are important features in gaining acceptance to recommendations. Which one of the following might be OVERLOOKED in preparing a report which is to have wide distribution?

    A. A comprehensive index
    B. An attractive binder
    C. Proper spacing and page layout
    D. Charts and tables

39. The elimination of meaningless reports, although reducing the total information output, IMPROVES the management process by

    A. determining the number of employees required to perform the work assigned
    B. identifying the difference between direct and indirect costs
    C. increasing the effectiveness of executives
    D. limiting the budget to variable costs

40. In determining whether or not to use a computerized system as opposed to a manual system, which of the following would normally have the MOST influence on the decision? The

    A. availability of analysts and programmers to design and install the system
    B. availability of computer time
    C. basic premise that all computerized systems are superior to manual systems
    D. volume and complexity of transactions required

KEY (CORRECT ANSWERS)

1. A	11. D	21. A	31. D
2. B	12. C	22. C	32. D
3. B	13. C	23. C	33. C
4. D	14. A	24. C	34. A
5. D	15. C	25. D	35. A
6. D	16. B	26. B	36. A
7. C	17. A	27. B	37. C
8. C	18. A	28. A	38. B
9. B	19. A	29. D	39. C
10. C	20. B	30. C	40. D

TEST 2

DIRECTIONS: Each question or incomplete statement is followed by several suggested answers or completions. Select the one that BEST answers the question or completes the statement. *PRINT THE LETTER OF THE CORRECT ANSWER IN THE SPACE AT THE RIGHT*

1. The one of the following that is NOT normally involved in the development of a management information system is

   A. determination of the best method of preparing and presenting the required information
   B. determination of line and staff relationships within the various units of the organizational structure
   C. determination of what specific information is needed for decision-making and control
   D. identification of the critical aspects of the business, i.e., the end results and other elements of performance which need to be planned and controlled

2. The long-term growth in size and complexity of both business and government has increased management's dependence on more formal written summaries of operating results in place of the informal, on-the-spot observations and judgments of smaller organizations.
   In addition, there is a growing management need to

   A. increase the complexity of those phases of the management process which have previously been simplified
   B. increase the speed and accuracy of artificial intelligence
   C. measure the effectiveness of managerial performance
   D. reduce alcoholism by greatly limiting personal contacts between the various levels of management within the organization

3. Of the following, it is MOST essential that a management information system provide information needed for

   A. determining computer time requirements
   B. developing new office layouts
   C. drawing new organization charts
   D. planning and measuring results

4. The PRIMARY purpose of control reports is to

   A. compare actual performance with planned results
   B. determine staffing requirements
   C. determine the work flow
   D. develop a new budget

5. Which one of the following has the GREATEST negative impact on communications in a large organization?

   A. Delays in formulating variable policies relating to communications
   B. Failure to conduct comprehensive courses in communications skills
   C. Failure to get information to those who need it
   D. Unclear organizational objectives

6. Efficiency of an organization is significantly impacted by all of the following EXCEPT

   A. network connectivity
   B. software compatibility
   C. hardware upgrades
   D. cloud data storage

7. The type of computer configuration in which the data are processed at one time after they have been made a matter of record is known as

   A. batching
   B. in line
   C. off line
   D. real time

8. A computer configuration system in which the input or output equipment is directly connected and operates under control of the computer is known as

   A. off line
   B. on line
   C. random access
   D. real time

9. A manager who wants to quickly analyze the output of a particular department would most likely refer to which one of the following?

   A. An Excel spreadsheet with production data logged by department
   B. Email reports submitted by department leaders
   C. Quarterly reports describing production targets and measurements
   D. An Excel spreadsheet with employee-generated survey data related to typical daily output and capabilities

10. Computers are generally considered to consist of four major sections. The one of the following which is NOT a major section is

   A. buffer
   B. control
   C. processing
   D. storage

11. Of the following, administrative control is PRIMARILY dependent upon

   A. adequate information
   B. a widespread spy network
   C. strict supervisors
   D. strong sanctions

12. Meticulous care must be exercised in writing the methodology section of the research report so that

   A. another investigator will achieve the same results if he repeats the study
   B. the interpretation of the findings cannot be challenged
   C. the report will be well balanced
   D. the rules of scientific logic are clearly indicated

13. When data are grouped into a frequency distribution, the *true mode* by definition is the _____ in the distribution.

   A. 50% point
   B. largest single range
   C. point of greatest concentration
   D. smallest single range

14. Which of the following is LEAST likely to be a potential benefit arising from the use of electronic data processing systems?

    A. Analysis of more data and analysis of data in greater depth than manual systems
    B. Increased speed and accuracy in information processing
    C. Lower capital expenditures for office equipment
    D. Reduced personnel costs in tabulating and reporting functions

15. A *grapevine* is BEST defined as

    A. a harmful method of communication
    B. a system of communication operative below the executive level
    C. an informal communication system of no functional importance to an organization
    D. the internal and non-systematic channel of communication within an organization

16. Of the following, the symbol shown at the right, as used in a systems flow chart, means

    A. document
    B. manual operation
    C. planning
    D. process

17. The mean age of a sample group drawn from population X is 37.5 years and the standard error of the mean is 5.9. There is a *99%* probability that the computed mean age of other samples drawn from population X would fall within the range of

    A. 31.6–43.4
    B. 26.0–52.7
    C. 22.2–52.8
    D. 20.0–55.0

18. After a budget has been developed, it serves to

    A. assist the accounting department in posting expenditures
    B. measure the effectiveness of department managers
    C. provide a yardstick against which actual costs are measured
    D. provide the operating department with total expenditures to date

19. In order to ensure that work measurement or time study results will be consistent from one study to another, and reflect a fair day's work, the performance of the clerks must be rated or levelled.
    Which of the following is LEAST likely to be included among the techniques for determining the performance level or for rating the study?

    A. Predetermined times
    B. Published rating tables
    C. Sampling studies
    D. Training films

20. Of the following, the BEST practice to follow when training a new employee is to

    A. encourage him to feel free to ask questions at any time
    B. immediately demonstrate how fast his job can be done so he will know what is expected of him
    C. let him watch other employees for a week or two
    D. point out mistakes after completion so he will learn by experience

21. An IMPORTANT aspect to keep in mind during the decision-making process is that

    A. all possible alternatives for attaining goals should be sought out and considered
    B. considering various alternatives only leads to confusion
    C. once a decision has been made, it cannot be retracted
    D. there is only one correct method to reach any goal

22. Implementation of accountability REQUIRES

    A. a leader who will not hesitate to take punitive action
    B. an established system of communication from the bottom to the top
    C. explicit directives from leaders
    D. too much expense to justify it

23. Of the following, the MAJOR difference between systems and procedures analysis and work simplification is:

    A. The former complicates organizational routine and the latter simplifies it
    B. The former is objective and the latter is subjective
    C. The former generally utilizes expert advice and the latter is a *do-it-yourself* improvement by supervisors and workers
    D. There is no difference other than in name

24. Systems development is concerned with providing

    A. a specific set of work procedures
    B. an overall framework to describe general relationships
    C. definitions of particular organizational functions
    D. organizational symbolism

25. Organizational systems and procedures should be

    A. developed as problems arise as no design can anticipate adequately the requirements of an organization
    B. developed jointly by experts in systems and procedures and the people who are responsible for implementing them
    C. developed solely by experts in systems and procedures
    D. eliminated whenever possible to save unnecessary expense

26. The CHIEF danger of a decentralized control system is that

    A. excessive reports and communications will be generated
    B. problem areas may not be detected readily
    C. the expense will become prohibitive
    D. this will result in too many *chiefs*

27. Of the following, management guides and controls clerical work PRINCIPALLY through

    A. close supervision and constant checking of personnel
    B. spot checking of clerical procedures
    C. strong sanctions for clerical supervisors
    D. the use of printed forms

28. Which of the following is MOST important before conducting fact-finding interviews?

A. Becoming acquainted with all personnel to be interviewed
B. Explaining the techniques you plan to use
C. Explaining to the operating officials the purpose and scope of the study
D. Orientation of the physical layout

29. Of the following, the one that is NOT essential in carrying out a comprehensive work improvement program is

A. standards of performance
B. supervisory training
C. work count/task list
D. work distribution chart

30. Which of the following control techniques is MOST useful on large, complex systems projects?

A. A general work plan
B. Gantt chart
C. Monthly progress report
D. PERT chart

31. The action which is MOST effective in gaining acceptance of a study by the agency which is being studied is

A. a directive from the agency head to install a study based on recommendations included in a report
B. a lecture-type presentation following approval of the procedures
C. a written procedure in narrative form covering the proposed system with visual presentations and discussions
D. procedural charts showing the *before* situation, forms, steps, etc. to the employees affected

32. Which of the following is NOT an advantage in the use of oral instructions as compared with written instructions? Oral instruction(s)

A. can easily be changed
B. is superior in transmitting complex directives
C. facilitate exchange of information between a superior and his subordinate
D. with discussions make it easier to ascertain understanding

33. Which organization principle is MOST closely related to procedural analysis and improvement?

A. Duplication, overlapping, and conflict should be eliminated.
B. Managerial authority should be clearly defined.
C. The objectives of the organization should be clearly defined.
D. Top management should be freed of burdensome detail.

34. Which one of the following is the MAJOR objective of operational audits?

A. Detecting fraud
B. Determining organization problems
C. Determining the number of personnel needed
D. Recommending opportunities for improving operating and management practices

35. Of the following, the formalization of organization structure is BEST achieved by

A. a narrative description of the plan of organization
B. functional charts
C. job descriptions together with organization charts
D. multi-flow charts

36. Budget planning is MOST useful when it achieves

A. cost control
B. forecast of receipts
C. performance review
D. personnel reduction

37. The UNDERLYING principle of sound administration is to

A. base administration on investigation of facts
B. have plenty of resources available
C. hire a strong administrator
D. establish a broad policy

38. Although questionnaires are not the best survey tool the management analyst has to use, there are times when a good questionnaire can expedite the *fact-finding* phase of a management survey.
Which of the following should be AVOIDED in the design and distribution of the questionnaire?

A. Questions should be framed so that answers can be classified and tabulated for analysis.
B. Those receiving the questionnaire must be knowledgeable enough to accurately provide the information desired.
C. The questionnaire should enable the respondent to answer in a narrative manner.
D. The questionnaire should require a minimum amount of writing.

39. Of the following, the formula which is used to calculate the arithmetic mean from data grouped in a frequency distribution is:
M =

A. $\frac{n}{\Sigma fx}$
B. $N(\Sigma fx)$
C. $\frac{\Sigma fx}{N}$
D. $\frac{\Sigma x}{fN}$

40. Arranging large groups of numbers in frequency distributions

A. gives a more composite picture of the total group than a random listing
B. is misleading in most cases
C. is unnecessary in most instances
D. presents the data in a form whereby further manipulation of the group is eliminated

KEY (CORRECT ANSWERS)

1. B	11. A	21. A	31. C
2. C	12. A	22. B	32. B
3. D	13. C	23. C	33. A
4. A	14. C	24. B	34. D
5. C	15. D	25. B	35. C
6. C	16. B	26. B	36. A
7. A	17. C	27. D	37. A
8. B	18. C	28. C	38. C
9. A	19. C	29. B	39. C
10. A	20. A	30. D	40. A

EXAMINATION SECTION

TEST 1

DIRECTIONS: Each question or incomplete statement is followed by several suggested answers or completions. Select the one that BEST answers the question or completes the statement. *PRINT THE LETTER OF THE CORRECT ANSWER IN THE SPACE AT THE RIGHT.*

1. In organizational theory, the optimum span of control, that is, the number of subordinates who can be effectively supervised by one man above the level of the first line supervisor is GENERALLY set at between 1.____
   A. 3 and 6 B. 6 and 12 C. 12 and 18 D. 18 and 24

2. Which of the following is LEAST desirable as a basic guide to normal conventional office layout? 2.____
   A. Arrange desks so that work flows in a normal fashion
   B. Place files nearest to the persons who will use them
   C. Utilize a number of small areas to provide privacy
   D. Utilize one single large area

3. *A set of objects together with relationships between the objects and between their attributes* is the definition of 3.____
   A. a perceptual whole and its subcomponents
   B. a system in the terms of specific systems theory
   C. an organism
   D. forms control

4. A technique of time study in which each employee maintains a record of his own time is GENERALLY known as _____ study. 4.____
   A. estimated time B. observed time
   C. time log D. wristwatch

5. An employee has approached a supervisor with a request for a change involving his personal status or with a suggestion for making an improvement in the work The supervisor knows that the suggestion cannot be granted. 5.____
   Of the following, the BEST procedure would be for the supervisor to
   A. refer the matter to the personnel department
   B. refer the matter to his superior for action
   C. reject the proposal, explaining the defects or objections which cannot be overcome
   D. shelve the idea so that the employee will realize it cannot be acted upon

6. There are, in general, a number of common methods of drawing samples for statistical work. 6.____
   The method in which a regularly ordered interval is maintained between the items chosen is BEST termed _____ sampling.
   A. random B. stratified or selective
   C. systematic D. work

7. The multi-column process chart can be put to all of the following general uses EXCEPT to 7.____
   A. improve office layout
   B. improve procedures
   C. standardize procedures
   D. train personnel

8. If one wished to show the percentage of change over a period of time, the MOST appropriate type of graph or chart GENERALLY would be the _____ chart. 8.____
   A. bar
   B. line or curve
   C. logarithmic or semilogarithmic
   D. pie

9. A chart designed for the explicit purpose of portraying graphically information relating to the degree of responsibility of key individuals for the performance of various functions is BEST described as a(n) _____ chart. 9.____
   A. linear responsibility
   B. work distribution
   C. work process
   D. staff

10. The technique of work measurement LEAST useful for setting up a program of office incentive pay GENERALLY would be 10.____
   A. log sheets
   B. stopwatch time study
   C. wristwatch time study
   D. work sampling

11. There are a number of steps to be taken in making a work sampling study in order to set production standards. Three of the steps listed below are peculiar only to work sampling, in contrast with other work measurement techniques. 11.____
   The one EXCEPTION is:
   A. Define the breakdown of work into the proper elements of work and no-work or delay to be observed
   B. Determine the required number of observations needed for the specified degree of reliability
   C. Establish the observation intervals
   D. Make a preliminary estimate of work and no-work or delay element percentages for step A

12. A number of standardized flow process chart symbols have been generally accepted. 12.____
   The symbol $\overline{\text{v}}$ GENERALLY indicates a(n)
   A. delay
   B. storage or file
   C. inspection
   D. operation

13. The number of standardized flow process chart symbols have been generally accepted. 13.____
   The symbol ▭ GENERALLY indicates a(n)
   A. delay
   B. storage or file
   C. inspection
   D. operation

14. The type of work for which short interval scheduling generally would be LEAST applicable would be the work of a group of 14.____
    A. calculating clerks
    B. order clerks
    C. technically-oriented clerks
    D. typists

15. In writing a business report, the BEST expression to use, in general, of those listed below would NORMALLY be: 15.____
    A. Because
    B. Inasmuch as
    C. In view of the fact that
    D. With reference to

16. Of the following, the MAJOR advantage of a random access data processing system, as compared with a sequential-type system, is its 16.____
    A. ability to use more than one input system
    B. demand for more sophisticated systems and programming
    C. greater storage capacity and access speed
    D. potential for processing data on a *first come, first-served* basis

17. A good rule to remember with regard to decision making is that decisions should be made 17.____
    A. at the highest level competent to make such a decision
    B. at the lowest level competent to make such a decision
    C. by the person responsible for carrying out the decision
    D. by the person responsible for the work of the unit

18. Which of the following potential systems would LEAST likely be improved by being online? A(n) _____ system. 18.____
    A. budgeting control
    B. welfare eligibility
    C. employee payroll
    D. inventory control

19. A management information and control system essentially should be designed to provide management personnel with up-to-date information which will enable them to improve control over their operations. 19.____
    In designing such a system, the FIRST step to determine is:
    A. What information is needed to effectively control operations?
    B. What information is presently available?
    C. What organization changes are necessary to implement the system?
    D. Who is presently processing the information that might be used?

20. In designing control reports, which of the following guidelines is of MOST importance? 20.____
    A. Financial information should always be carried to the nearest penny.
    B. The report should be a simple and concise statement of only the pertinent facts.
    C. The report should indicate the source of original data and how the computations were made.
    D. The report should have the broadest possible distribution at all levels of management.

21. A situation which enables a number of users at offsite locations to have access to an office computer network is called 21.____
    A. multiprocessing B. multiprogramming
    C. cloud connectivity D. remote access

22. Computer software that would typically be used for widespread dissemination of a business report is 22.____
    A. Microsoft Word B. Microsoft PowerPoint
    C. Adobe Elements D. Google Sheets

23. Which of the following steps is LEAST desirable in designing an electronic data processing system? 23.____
    A. Design the EDP system first, then relate it to current operations
    B. Develop a corollary chart for the corresponding flow of information
    C. Develop a flow chart for the functions affected by the system
    D. Obtain from available EDP equipment that which best fits current operations

24. Electronic data processing equipment can produce more information faster than can be generated by any other means. Because this is true, one wonders whether our ability to generate information has not far outstripped our ability to assimilate it. 24.____
    In view of this, a PERSISTENT danger management faces is in
    A. determining the budget for management information systems
    B. determining what information is of real worth
    C. finding enough computer personnel
    D. keeping their computers fully occupied

25. The one of the following that is an ADVANTAGE of a hybrid local/remote network setup over fully local access is 25.____
    A. the ability to access a network outside normal circumstances
    B. closer oversight of personnel
    C. more efficient workflow
    D. reduced costs for software and production equipment

KEY (CORRECT ANSWERS)

1.	A	11.	A
2.	C	12.	B
3.	A	13.	C
4.	C	14.	C
5.	C	15.	A
6.	C	16.	D
7.	A	17.	B
8.	C	18.	C
9.	A	19.	A
10.	A	20.	B

21.	D
22.	A
23.	A
24.	B
25.	A

TEST 2

DIRECTIONS: Each question or incomplete statement is followed by several suggested answers or completions. Select the one that BEST answers the question or completes the statement. *PRINT THE LETTER OF THE CORRECT ANSWER IN THE SPACE AT THE RIGHT.*

1. In analyzing data for the acquisition of new equipment, an analyst gathers the facts, analyzes them, and develops new procedures which will be required when the new equipment arrives. 1.____
   Inn analyzing the factors involved, which one of the following is normally LEAST important in the evaluation of new equipment?
   A. Cost factors
   B. Layout and installation factors
   C. Production planning
   D. Operational experience of manufacturers of allied equipment

2. If an analyst is required to recommend the selection of a machine for an office operation, he can BEST judge the expected output of a particular machine by pursuing which of the following courses of action? 2.____
   Obtain
   A. an actual test run of the machine in his office
   B. data from the manufacturer of the machine
   C. information on the percentage of working time the machine will be used
   D. the experience of actual users of similar machines elsewhere

3. Of the following, the BEST definition of records management is 3.____
   A. storage of all types of records at minimum expense
   B. planned control of all types of records
   C. storage of records for maximum accessibility
   D. systematic filing of all types of records

4. The one of the following which is NOT a primary objective of a records retention and disposal system is to 4.____
   A. assure appropriate preservation of records having permanent value
   B. dispose of records not warranting further preservation
   C. establish retention standards for archives
   D. provide an opportunity to use miniaturization

5. Of the following functions of management, the one which should NORMALLY precede the others is 5.____
   A. coordinating B. directing C. organizing D. planning

6. One of the more famous studies of organizations is called the Hawthorne study. 6.____
   This work was one of the first to point out the importance of
   A. employee's benefit and retirement programs
   B. informal organization among employees
   C. job engineering
   D. styles of position classification

7. In organization theory, the type of position in which an individual is appointed to give technical aid to management on a particular problem area is generally BEST termed a(n) 7.____
   A. administrative assistant
   B. assistant to
   C. staff assistant
   D. staff specialist

8. In organizing, doing what works in the particular situation, with due regard to both short- and long-range objective, is BEST termed 8.____
   A. ambivalence
   B. authoritarianism
   C. decentralization
   D. pragmatism

9. If an effort were made to reduce the number of private offices in a new layout, the LEAST effective substitute in offering privacy would be the use of 9.____
   A. an open area with lower movable partitions or railings separating each individual
   B. conference rooms
   C. larger desks
   D. modular desk units

10. The term *administrative substation* NORMALLY refers to 10.____
    A. a work station handling a number of office services for an office organization
    B. a work station where middle level supervisors are located
    C. an office for handling management trainees
    D. the functions allocated to particular levels of administrative managers

11. An operations research technique which would be applied to determine the optimum number of window clerks or interviewers to have in an agency serving the public would MOST likely be the use of 11.____
    A. line of balance
    B. queuing theory
    C. simulation
    D. work sampling

12. A type of file which permits the operator to remain seated while the file can be moved backward and forward as required is BEST termed a _____ file. 12.____
    A. lateral
    B. movable
    C. reciprocating
    D. rotary

13. The technique of work measurement in which the analyst observes the work at random times of the day is BEST termed 13.____
    A. indirect observation
    B. logging
    C. ratio delay
    D. wristwatch

14. Examples of predetermined time systems generally should include all of the following EXCEPT 14.____
    A. Master Clerical Data
    B. Methods Time Measurement
    C. Short Interval Data
    D. Work Factor

15. A technique by which the supervisor or an assistant distributes a predetermined batch of work to the employee at periodic intervals of the day is generally BEST known as 15.____
    A. backlog control scheduling
    B. production control scheduling
    C. short interval schedule
    D. workload balancing

16. E. Wright Bakke defined his *fusion process* as: The 16.____
    A. work environment to some degree remakes the organization and the organization to some degree remakes the work environment
    B. fusing of the interests of both management and labor unions
    C. community of interest between first line supervisors and top management
    D. organization to some degree remakes the individual and the individual to some degree remakes the organization

17. A pamphlet on issues related to 2020s-era office setup would likely be titled 17.____
    A. Close Encounters: How Proximity Elevates Production
    B. How Connectivity Spurs Inspiration
    C. See Your Employees in a New Light With Open Floor Plans
    D. From A to Zoom: The Terminology of the Hybrid Workplace

18. In planning office space for a newly established bureau, it would usually be LEAST desirable to 18.____
    A. concentrate, rather than disperse, the chief sources of office noises
    B. design an office environment with the same brightness as the office desk
    C. designate as reception rooms, washrooms, and other service areas those areas that will receive lesser amounts of illumination than those areas in which private office work will be performed
    D. eliminate natural light in cases where it is not the major light source

19. A private office should be used when its use is dictated by facts and unbiased judgment. It should never be provided simply because requests and sometimes pressure have been brought to bear. 19.____
    Of the following reasons used to justify use of a private office, the one that requires the MOST care in determining whether a private office is actually warranted is
    A. an office has always been provided for a particular job
    B. prestige considerations
    C. the confidential nature of the work
    D. the work involves high concentration

20. Theoretically, an ideal organization structure can be set up for each enterprise. In actual practice, the ideal organization structure is seldom, if ever, obtained. 20.____
    Of the following, the one that normally is of LEAST influence in determining the organization structure is the
    A. existence of agreements and favors among members of the organization
    B. funds available
    C. opinions and beliefs of top executives
    D. tendency of management to discard established forms in favor of new forms

21. An IMPORTANT aspect to keep in mind during the decision-making process is that 21.____
    A. all possible alternatives for attaining goals should be sought out and considered
    B. considering various alternatives only leads to confusion
    C. once a decision has been made, it cannot be retracted
    D. there is only one correct method to reach any goal

22. Implementation of accountability requires 22.____
    A. a leader who will not hesitate to take punitive action
    B. an established system of communication from the bottom to the top
    C. explicit directives from leaders
    D. too much expense to justify it

23. Of the following, the MAJOR difference between systems and procedures analysis and work simplification is: 23.____
    A. The former complicates organizational routine and the latter simplifies it
    B. The former is objective and the latter is subjective
    C. The former generally utilizes expert advice and the latter is a *do-it-yourself* improvement by supervisors and workers
    D. There is no difference other than in name

24. Systems development is concerned with providing 24.____
    A. a specific set of work procedures
    B. an overall framework to describe general relationships
    C. definitions of particular organizational functions
    D. organizational symbolism

25. Organizational systems and procedures should be 25.____
    A. developed as problems arise as no design can anticipate adequately the requirements of an organization
    B. developed jointly by experts in systems and procedures and the people who are responsible for implementing them
    C. developed solely by experts in systems and procedures
    D. eliminated whenever possible to save unnecessary expense

KEY (CORRECT ANSWERS)

1. D
2. A
3. B
4. D
5. D

6. B
7. D
8. D
9. C
10. A

11. B
12. C
13. C
14. C
15. C

16. D
17. D
18. D
19. A
20. D

21. A
22. B
23. C
24. B
25. B

TEST 3

DIRECTIONS: Each question or incomplete statement is followed by several suggested answers or completions. Select the one that BEST answers the question or completes the statement. *PRINT THE LETTER OF THE CORRECT ANSWER IN THE SPACE AT THE RIGHT.*

1. The CHIEF danger of a decentralized control system is that 1.____
   A. excessive reports and communications will be generated
   B. problem areas may not be detected readily
   C. the expense will become routine
   D. this will result in too many *chiefs*

2. Of the following, management guides and controls clerical work PRINCIPALLY through 2.____
   A. close supervision and constant checking of personnel
   B. spot checking of clerical procedures
   C. strong sanctions for clerical supervisors
   D. the use of printed forms

3. Which of the following is MOST important before conducting fact-finding interviews? 3.____
   A. Becoming acquainted with all personnel to be interviewed
   B. Explaining the techniques you plan to use
   C. Explaining to the operating officials the purpose and scope of the study
   D. Orientation of the physical layout

4. Of the following, the one that is NOT essential in carrying out a comprehensive work improvement program is 4.____
   A. standards of performance
   B. supervisory training
   C. work count/task list
   D. work distribution chart

5. Which of the following control techniques is MOST useful on large complex systems projects? 5.____
   A. A general work plan
   B. Gantt chart
   C. Monthly progress report
   D. PERT chart

6. The action which is MOST effective in gaining acceptance of a study by the agency which is being studied is 6.____
   A. a directive from the agency head to install a study based on recommendations included in a report
   B. a lecture-type presentation following approval of the procedures
   C. a written procedure in narrative form covering the proposed system with visual presentations and discussions
   D. procedural charts showing the *before* situation, forms, steps, etc. to the employees affected

7. Which of the following is NOT an advantage in the use of oral instructions as compared with written instructions? Oral instruction(s) 7.____
   A. can easily be changed
   B. is superior in transmitting complex directives
   C. facilitate exchange of information between a superior and his subordinate
   D. with discussions make it easier to ascertain understanding

8. Which organization principle is MOST closely related to procedural analysis and improvement? 8.____
   A. Duplication, overlapping, and conflict should be eliminated.
   B. Managerial authority should be clearly defined.
   C. The objectives of the organization should be clearly defined.
   D. Top management should be freed of burdensome detail.

9. Which one of the following is the MAJOR objective of operational audits? 9.____
   A. Detecting fraud
   B. Determining organization problems
   C. Determining the number of personnel needed
   D. Recommending opportunities for improving operating and management practices

10. Of the following, the formalization of organization structure is BEST achieved by 10.____
   A. a narrative description of the plan of organization
   B. functional charts
   C. job descriptions together with organization charts
   D. multi-flow charts

11. Budget planning is MOST useful when it achieves 11.____
   A. cost control
   B. forecast of receipts
   C. performance review
   D. personnel reduction

12. The UNDERLYING principle of sound administration is to 12.____
   A. base administration on investigation facts
   B. have plenty of resources available
   C. hire a strong administrator
   D. establish a broad policy

13. Although questionnaires are not the best survey tool the management analyst has to use, there are times when a good questionnaire can expedite the *fact-finding* phase of a management survey. 13.____
Which of the following should be AVOIDED in the design and distribution of the questionnaire?
   A. Questions should be framed so that answers can be classified and tabulated for analysis.
   B. Those receiving the questionnaire must be knowledgeable enough to accurately provide the information desired.

C. The questionnaire should enable the respondent to answer in a narrative manner.
D. The questionnaire should require a minimum amount of writing.

14. Of the following, the formula which is used to calculate the arithmetic mean from data grouped in a frequency distribution is M = 14.____

A. $\frac{N}{\Sigma fx}$ B. $N(\Sigma fx)$ C. $\frac{\Sigma fx}{N}$ D. $\frac{\Sigma x}{fN}$

15. Arranging large groups of numbers in frequency distributions 15.____
A. gives a more composite picture of the total group than a random listing
B. is misleading in most cases
C. is unnecessary in most instances
D. presents the data in a form whereby further manipulation of the group is eliminated

16. After a budget has been developed, it serves to 16.____
A. assist the accounting department in posting expenditures
B. measure the effectiveness of department managers
C. provide a yardstick against which actual costs are measured
D. provide the operating department with total expenditure to date

17. Of the following, which formula is used to determine staffing requirements? 17.____

A. $\frac{\text{Hours per man-day}}{\text{Volume x Standard}}$ = Employees Needed

B. $\frac{\text{Hours per man-day x Standard}}{\text{Volume}}$ = Employees Needed

C. $\frac{\text{Hours per man-day x Volume}}{\text{Standard}}$ = Employees Needed

D. $\frac{\text{Volume x Standard}}{\text{Hours per man-day}}$ = Employees Needed

18. Of the following, which formula is used to determine the number of days required to process work? 18.____

A. $\frac{\text{Employees x Daily Output}}{\text{Volume}}$ = Days to Process Work

B. $\frac{\text{Employees x Volume}}{\text{Daily Output}}$ = Days to Process Work

C. $\frac{\text{Volume}}{\text{Employees x Daily Output}}$ = Days to Process Work

D. $\frac{\text{Volume x Daily Output}}{\text{Employees}}$ = Days to Process Work

19. Identify this symbol, as used in a Systems Flow Chart. 19.____
    A. Document
    B. Decision
    C. Preparation
    D. Process

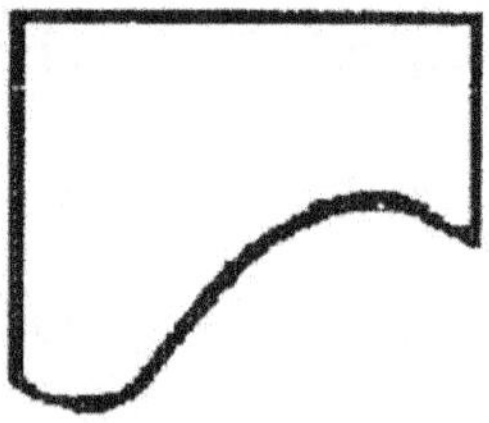

20. Of the following, the MAIN advantage of a form letter over a dictated letter is that a form letter 20.____
    A. is more expressive
    B. is neater
    C. may be mailed in a window envelope
    D. requires less secretarial time

21. The term that may be defined as a *systematic analysis of all factors affecting work being done or all factors that will affect work to be done, in order to save effort, time, or money* is 21.____
    A. flow process charting
    B. work flow analysis
    C. work measurement
    D. work simplification

22. Generally, the LEAST important basic factor to be considered in developing office layout improvements is to locate 22.____
    A. office equipment, reference facilities, and files as close as practicable to those using them
    B. persons as close as practicable to the persons from whom they receive their work
    C. persons as close as practicable to windows and/or adequate ventilation
    D. persons who are friendly with each other close together to improve morale

23. Of the following, the one which is LEAST effective in reducing administrative costs is 23.____
    A. applying objective measurement techniques to determine the time required to perform a given task
    B. establishing budgets on the basis of historical performance data
    C. motivating supervisors and managers in the importance of cost reduction
    D. selecting the best method—manual, mechanical, or electronic—to process the essential work

24. *Fire-fighting* is a common expression in management terminology. 24.____
    Of the following, which BEST describes *fire-fighting* as an analyst's approach to solving paperwork problems?
    A. A complete review of all phases of the department's processing functions
    B. A studied determination of the proper equipment to process the work
    C. An analysis of each form that is being processed and the logical reasons for its processing
    D. The solution of problems as they arise, usually at the request of operating personnel

25. Assume that an analyst with a proven record of accomplishment on many projects is having difficulties on his present assignment. 25.____
Of the following, the BEST course of action for his superior to take is to
   A. assume there is a personality conflict involved and transfer the analyst to another project
   B. give the analyst some time off
   C. review the nature of the project to determine whether or not the analyst is equipped to handle the assignment
   D. suggest that the analyst seek counseling

KEY (CORRECT ANSWERS)

1.	B	11.	A
2.	D	12.	A
3.	C	13.	C
4.	B	14.	C
5.	D	15.	A
6.	C	16.	C
7.	B	17.	D
8.	A	18.	C
9.	D	19.	A
10.	C	20.	D

21.	D
22.	D
23.	B
24.	D
25.	C

EXAMINATION SECTION
TEST 1

DIRECTIONS: Each question or incomplete statement is followed by several suggested answers or completions. Select the one that BEST answers the question or completes the statement. *PRINT THE LETTER OF THE CORRECT ANSWER IN THE SPACE AT THE RIGHT.*

1. What type of reinforcement schedule is illustrated by a sales commission? 1.____

   A. Variable interval
   B. Variable ratio
   C. Fixed interval
   D. Fixed ratio

2. Mathematical models of management grew out of the ______ school of management. 2.____

   A. behavioral
   B. systems
   C. contingency
   D. scientific

3. *Individual equity* is the term for the extent to which 3.____

   A. pay rates allocated to specific individuals within the organization reflect variations in individual merit
   B. pay rates for particular jobs correspond to rates paid for similar jobs on the entire job market
   C. pay rates for various jobs inside the organization reflect the relative worth of those jobs
   D. compensable factors will be used to rate the worth of particular jobs

4. External audits of a company are normally performed every 4.____

   A. month
   B. quarter
   C. year
   D. two years

5. Production design is primarily concerned with ______ controls. 5.____

   A. marginal
   B. process
   C. input
   D. output

6. The use of profit centers is appropriate only when 6.____

   A. it is used to measure the direct profit impact of the unit's efforts
   B. the unit is responsible for revenues, but does not have control over costs of the products they handle
   C. the unit has significant control over both costs and revenues
   D. the unit has control over investment decisions

7. A human resource manager's attention should be focused *primarily* on ______ during managerial selection. 7.____

   A. job behavior
   B. education level
   C. interview results
   D. test scores

8. Which of the following computer–based information systems would be used to handle word processing? 8.____

   A. TPS
   B. MIS
   C. OAS
   D. DSS

9. The technique most useful for solving inventory problems is 9.____

A. the Delphi technique
B. EOQ
C. queuing
D. linear programming

10. A commission formed by a company is responsible to 10.____

A. the general public
B. top–level management
C. union leaders
D. stockholders

11. Each of the following is typically considered an ordering cost EXCEPT 11.____

A. time
B. paperwork
C. pilferage
D. postage

12. The use of scenarios may help managers to 12.____

A. tighten day–to–day control
B. examine different possible outcomes
C. lengthen their reaction times
D. anticipate the unknowable

13. During the appraisal of an employee's performance, a human resources manager tends to compare the employee with other coworkers, rather than with a performance standard. What type of rating error is occurring? 13.____

A. Severity error
B. Contrast error
C. Halo effect
D. Recency error

14. A supervisor rates a subordinate's initiative in an evaluation. This is an example of a(n) _______ measure. 14.____

A. cognitive
B. emotional
C. qualitative
D. quantitative

15. A _______ budget is NOT an operating budget. 15.____

A. profit
B. cash
C. expense
D. sales

16. Which of the following is a characteristic of a dynamic, complex company environment? 16.____

A. Predictability
B. Minimal need of sophisticated knowledge
C. Numerous products and services
D. Stability

17. A management information system is capable of each of the following EXCEPT 17.____

A. making unprogrammed decisions
B. providing early warning signals
C. aiding decision–making
D. automating clerical functions

18. In reinforcement theory, a technique that involves withholding previously available positive consequences associated with a behavior, in order to *decrease* that behavior, is known as 18.____

    A. negative reinforcement
    B. shaping
    C. punishment
    D. extinction

19. Which of the following is NOT a disadvantage associated with highly specialized, low–discretion jobs? 19.____

    A. Failing to utilize employee intelligence
    B. Can result in unproductive behaviors
    C. Requiring hiring highly trained, more expensive labor
    D. Is inconsistent with values and lifestyles of employees

20. Which of the following is an example of a line department? 20.____

    A. Production
    B. Finance
    C. Accounting
    D. Research and development

21. A computer–based OAS system is intended *primarily* to 21.____

    A. execute routine transactions
    B. allow access to historic information
    C. improve the decision–making process
    D. facilitate communication

22. The process of acquainting new employees with the policies and standards of the company is known as 22.____

    A. recruitment
    B. orientation
    C. staffing
    D. development

23. What is the term for the process of planning how to match supply with product or service demand over a time horizon of approximately one year? 23.____

    A. Capacity planning
    B. Forecasting
    C. Aggregate production planning
    D. Capacity requirements planning

24. Authority is correctly defined as the 24.____

    A. right to command and allocate resources
    B. accountability for achievement of goals and the efficient use of resources
    C. ability to influence others and control resources
    D. tendency to delegate tasks

25. According to situational leadership theory, when subordinates are able and willing to take appropriate responsibility, the appropriate leadership action is 25.____

    A. telling
    B. selling
    C. delegating
    D. participating

KEY (CORRECT ANSWERS)

1. D
2. D
3. A
4. C
5. C
6. C
7. A
8. C
9. B
10. A
11. C
12. B
13. B
14. C
15. B
16. C
17. A
18. D
19. C
20. A
21. D
22. B
23. C
24. A
25. C

TEST 2

DIRECTIONS: Each question or incomplete statement is followed by several suggested answers or completions. Select the one that BEST answers the question or completes the statement. *PRINT THE LETTER OF THE CORRECT ANSWER IN THE SPACE AT THE RIGHT.*

1. Formalized job rotation programs are an example of 1.____

   A. training
   B. career pathing
   C. recruitment
   D. career counseling

2. A(n) ______ is an example of a process layout pattern. 2.____

   A. automobile assembly line
   B. food processing plant
   C. department store
   D. hospital

3. Which of the following is MOST likely to be an output from a computerized decision support system? 3.____

   A. Projections
   B. Summary reports
   C. Special reports
   D. Schedules

4. When a company's replacement ratio is too high, 4.____

   A. replacement costs are too high
   B. there has been blocking of lower–level personnel
   C. insufficient weeding out has taken place
   D. a shortage of capable managers exists

5. An advantage associated with functional job grouping is that it 5.____

   A. facilitates organizational growth
   B. allows for easier hiring
   C. makes allocation of expenses easier
   D. facilitates coordination of top managers

6. Which of the following is an advantage associated with group decision–making? 6.____

   A. Choice of best alternative
   B. Less time–consuming
   C. Encouragement of innovative thinking
   D. Lower cost

7. On an organization chart, a solid line represents a(n) 7.____

   A. vertically integrated distribution channel
   B. indirect authority relationship
   C. horizontally integrated distribution channel
   D. line authority relationship

8. Which type of power, if exercised by a manager, is most likely to secure the commitment of subordinates? 8.____

   A. Legitimate
   B. Reward
   C. Information
   D. Referent

9. Which functional area of a company involves employee relations? 9.____

A. Finance
B. Marketing
C. Operations
D. Development

10. In a restaurant, a manager tallies the number of meals that are served within 15 minutes of the customer orders. Which type of statistical quality control measure is the manager using? 10.____

A. Input
B. Marginal
C. Attribute
D. Variable

11. Low–level analysis is most likely to be processed by which of the following kinds of computer information systems? 11.____

A. TPS
B. DSS
C. OAS
D. MIS

12. Of the following, bottom–up budgeting best incorporates 12.____

A. information on markets
B. company planning parameters
C. corporate goals
D. industry projections

13. A worker experiences role ____________ when his/her role within the organization is unclear. 13.____

A. discord
B. confusion
C. ambiguity
D. conflict

14. Which of the following is a DISADVANTAGE associated with the use of pay as an enforcer of employee performance? 14.____

A. Time lag
B. Low employee value
C. Unequal pay among employees
D. Erosion of value due to inflation

15. A company forms a temporary task force to study a problem in the community, and the company's relationship to that problem. In terms of forming responses to social issues, the company is practicing 15.____

A. implicit change
B. structural change
C. tokenism
D. functional change

16. A manager cannot assign probabilities to outcomes because he lacks information. The manager is said to be making a decision under the condition of 16.____

A. peril
B. certainty
C. uncertainty
D. risk

17. Using the resource dependence approach to controls, a manager determines that her unit is highly dependent on another unit for a particular resource, and that the expected resource flows are unacceptable. It is also determined, however, that the control process is probably not feasible for her department. 17.____
The manager should

A. do nothing
B. research a way to lower costs
C. develop alternatives to control
D. initiate the control process and try to adjust as it progresses

18. In the path–goal theory of leadership, the monitoring and control aspects of a leader's behavior are examples of ______ behavior. 18.____

A. participative
B. supportive
C. instrumental
D. goal–oriented

19. When a particular task is simple and morale is not an issue, ______ communication is probably the best method. 19.____

A. circle
B. chain
C. wheel
D. all–channel

20. In production and operations control, establishing a wage and salary structure is a function of 20.____

A. production planning
B. production design
C. production evaluation
D. selection

21. Which of the following is a type of inventory that consists of raw materials, components, and subassemblies that are used in the production of an end product or service? 21.____

A. Dependent demand inventory
B. Bill of materials
C. Independent demand inventory
D. Cost inventory

22. ______ job testing is a means of measuring mainly mental, mechanical, and clerical capacities. 22.____

A. Personality
B. Ability
C. Performance
D. Replacement

23. Historically, the management theory that first emphasized the need for companies to operate in a rational manner rather than according to the whims of owners and managers was the theory of ______ management. 23.____

A. behaviorist
B. quantitative
C. administrative
D. bureaucratic

24. Which of the following is an example of *discretionary* costs? 24.____

A. Raw materials
B. Mortgages
C. Sales commissions
D. Accounting fees

25. According to the systems approach to management, a system that operates in continual interaction with its environment is a(n) ______ system. 25.____

A. open B. feedback C. charged D. looped

KEY (CORRECT ANSWERS)

1.	A	11.	D
2.	C	12.	A
3.	C	13.	C
4.	B	14.	A
5.	B	15.	D
6.	A	16.	C
7.	D	17.	C
8.	D	18.	C
9.	C	19.	C
10.	C	20.	B

21. A
22. B
23. D
24. D
25. A

TEST 3

DIRECTIONS: Each question or incomplete statement is followed by several suggested answers or completions. Select the one that BEST answers the question or completes the statement. *PRINT THE LETTER OF THE CORRECT ANSWER IN THE SPACE AT THE RIGHT.*

1. In a complex organization, the process of differentiation is likely to create problems associated with 1.____

   A. controlling size
   B. management training
   C. coordination
   D. motivation

2. Before a company can determine whether a management information system can be developed, a(n) _______ must be performed. 2.____

   A. algorithm
   B. organizational chart
   C. feasibility study
   D. conversion

3. Job testing is considered to be reliable when 3.____

   A. a good test score is a clear predictor of job success
   B. the test measures what it professes to measure
   C. the test is clearly related to the job
   D. the candidate would earn roughly the same score if the test were repeated

4. A control system that is self–regulating is said to be 4.____

   A. formalized
   B. feedback–looped
   C. cybernetic
   D. centralized

5. A company with many rules and procedures is usually described as having a(n) _______ span of control. 5.____

   A. almost nonexistent
   B. narrow
   C. moderate
   D. wide

6. Altogether, the various types of financial statements are considered _______ control. 6.____

   A. input
   B. output
   C. process
   D. steering

7. A human resources manager teaches a new employee what to do, where to go for help, and what the company's important rules and policies are. What stage of orientation is being transacted? 7.____

   A. Implementation
   B. Socialization
   C. Induction
   D. Evaluation

8. The factors necessary in order to estimate partial–factor productivity are _______ and goods/services produced. 8.____

   A. labor hours
   B. labor hours, capital,
   C. capital, energy, materials,
   D. labor hours, capital, energy, technology, materials,

9. A company's _______ policy will decide the channels of distribution for a given product. 9.____

   A. financial
   B. personnel
   C. marketing
   D. product

10. Which of the following factors favors decentralization of computerized information system resources? 10.____

A. Increasing availability of user–friendly software
B. Staff specialization
C. Easier control of corporate databases
D. Potential for economies of scale

11. Each of the following typically helps implement authority in an organization EXCEPT 11.____

A. span of control
B. centralization
C. chain of command
D. familiarity

12. A maintenance goal 12.____

A. implies a specific level of activity over time
B. expresses the hope for growth
C. uses action verbs to indicate change
D. implies an effort to reorganize

13. Each of the following is a potential pitfall associated with financial controls EXCEPT 13.____

A. neglecting to link controls to strategic planning process
B. stifling innovation and creativity
C. not sophisticated enough for organizational needs
D. mixed messages about desired behaviors

14. The term for a statement of the skills, abilities, education, and previous work experience required to perform a particular job is the 14.____

A. replacement chart
B. job specification
C. job description
D. job analysis

15. The most successful use of the practice of job rotation is 15.____

A. to create maximum flexibility through cross–training
B. as an employee development tool
C. to alleviate boredom with simple jobs
D. to improve departmental loyalty

16. A company vice president delegates the authority to make a decision to a product manager. This is an example of 16.____

A. outsourcing
B. horizontal decentralization
C. vertical decentralization
D. centralized decision–making

17. Time–and–motion studies were first carried out by the ______ school of management. 17.____

A. scientific
B. human relations
C. classical
D. contingency

18. What is the term for the dispersion of organizational power? 18.____

A. Unity of command
B. Span of control
C. Formalization
D. Decentralization

19. _______ is the term for a technique to enhance creativity that relies on analogies. 19.____

A. Storming
B. Entropy
C. Cybernetics
D. Synectics

20. Which of the following is NOT considered to be a limitation associated with organization charts? 20.____

A. May not indicate real power and influence of people on the chart
B. Does not show a picture of the structure at a particular point in time
C. Frequently outdated
D. May not show actual formal relationships

21. Which of the following is considered to be a *snapshot* of an organization at a particular point in time? 21.____

A. Expense budget
B. Income statement
C. Balance sheet
D. Cash flow statement

22. Each of the following would be considered a safety and security need for an employee EXCEPT 22.____

A. merit pay raises
B. job security
C. pay raises references to the cost of living
D. benefits

23. The behavioral model of management contributed the idea of 23.____

A. quantitative aids for decision–making
B. organization members as active human resources
C. the potential importance of the environment to organizational success
D. the need for a scientific approach to management

24. According to the contingency perspective, which of the following would NOT be a major contingency factor for a business? 24.____

A. Strategy
B. Size
C. External environment
D. Technology in use

25. Which of the following is NOT an example of a single–use plan? 25.____

A. Standing plan
B. Budget
C. Project
D. Program

KEY (CORRECT ANSWERS)

1. B
2. C
3. D
4. C
5. D
6. B
7. C
8. A
9. C
10. A
11. D
12. A
13. C
14. B
15. B
16. C
17. C
18. D
19. D
20. B
21. C
22. A
23. B
24. B
25. A

PRINCIPLES AND PRACTICES, OF ADMINISTRATION, SUPERVISION AND MANAGEMENT

TABLE OF CONTENTS

PRINCIPLES AND PRACTICES, OF ADMINISTRATION, SUPERVISION AND MANAGEMENT

Most people are inclined to think of administration as something that only a few persons are responsible for in a large organization. Perhaps this is true if you are thinking of Administration with a capital *A*, but administration with a lower case *a* is a responsibility of supervisors at all levels each working day.

All of us feel we are pretty good supervisors and that we do a good job of administering the workings of our agency. By and large, this is true, but every so often it is good to check up on ourselves. Checklists appear from time to time in various publications which psychologists say tell whether or not a person will make a good wife, husband, doctor, lawyer, or supervisor.

The following questions are an excellent checklist to test yourself as a supervisor and administrator.

Remember, Administration gives direction and points the way but administration carries the ideas to fruition. Each is dependent on the other for its success. Remember, too, that no unit is too small for these departmental functions to be carried out. These statements apply equally as well to the Chief Librarian as to the Department Head with but one or two persons to supervise.

GENERAL ADMINISTRATION: General Responsibilities of Supervisors

1. Have I prepared written statements of functions, activities, and duties for my organizational unit?

2. Have I prepared procedural guides for operating activities?

3. Have I established clearly in writing, lines of authority and responsibility for my organizational unit?

4. Do I make recommendations for improvements in organization, policies, administrative and operating routines and procedures, including simplification of work and elimination of non-essential operations?

5. Have I designated and trained an understudy to function in my absence?

6. Do I supervise and train personnel within the unit to effectively perform their assignments?

7. Do I assign personnel and distribute work on such a basis as to carry out the organizational unit's assignment or mission in the most effective and efficient manner?

8. Have I established administrative controls by:

    a. Fixing responsibility and accountability on all supervisors under my direction for the proper performance of their functions and duties.

b. Preparations and submitting periodic work load and progress reports covering the operations of the unit to my immediate superior.

c. Analysis and evaluation of such reports received from subordinate units.

d. Submission of significant developments and problems arising within the organizational unit to my immediate superior.

e. Conducting conferences, inspections, etc., as to the status and efficiency of unit operations.

9. Do I maintain an adequate and competent working force?

10. Have I fostered good employee-department relations, seeing that established rules, regulations, and instructions are being carried out properly?

11. Do I collaborate and consult with other organizational units performing related functions to insure harmonious and efficient working relationships?

12. Do I maintain liaison through prescribed channels with city departments and other governmental agencies concerned with the activities of the unit?

13. Do I maintain contact with and keep abreast of the latest developments and techniques of administration (professional societies, groups, periodicals, etc.) as to their applicability to the activities of the unit?

14. Do I communicate with superiors and subordinates through prescribed organizational channels?

15. Do I notify superiors and subordinates in instances where bypassing is necessary as soon thereafter as practicable?

16. Do I keep my superior informed of significant developments and problems?

SEVEN BASIC FUNCTIONS OF THE SUPERVISOR

I. PLANNING
This means working out goals and means to obtain goals. What needs to be done, who will do it, how, when, and where it is to be done.

SEVEN STEPS IN PLANNING

A. Define job or problem clearly.
B. Consider priority of job.
C. Consider time-limit—starting and completing.
D. Consider minimum distraction to, or interference with, other activities.
E. Consider and provide for contingencies—possible emergencies.
F. Break job down into components.

G. Consider the 5 W's and H:
WHY..........is it necessary to do the job? (Is the purpose clearly defined?)
WHAT........needs to be done to accomplish the defined purpose?
.........is needed to do the job? (Money, materials, etc.)
WHO..........is needed to do the job?
..........will have responsibilities?
WHERE......is the work to be done?
WHEN........is the job to begin and end? (Schedules, etc.)
HOW..........is the job to bed done? (Methods, controls, records, etc.)

II. ORGANIZING

This means dividing up the work, establishing clear lines of responsibility and authority and coordinating efforts to get the job done.

III. STAFFING

The whole personnel function of bringing in and training staff, getting the right man and fitting him to the right job—the job to which he is best suited.

In the normal situation, the supervisor's responsibility regarding staffing normally includes providing accurate job descriptions, that is, duties of the jobs, requirements, education and experience, skills, physical, etc.; assigning the work for maximum use of skills; and proper utilization of the probationary period to weed out unsatisfactory employees.

IV. DIRECTING

Providing the necessary leadership to the group supervised. Important work gets done to the supervisor's satisfaction.

V. COORDINATING

The all-important duty of inter-relating the various parts of the work.
The supervisor is also responsible for controlling the coordinated activities. This means measuring performance according to a time schedule and setting quotas to see that the goals previously set are being reached. Reports from workers should be analyzed, evaluated, and made part of all future plans.

VI. REPORTING

This means proper and effective communication to your superiors, subordinates, and your peers (in definition of the job of the supervisor). Reports should be read and information contained therein should be used, not be filed away and forgotten. Reports should be written in such a way that the desired action recommended by the report is forthcoming.

VII. BUDGETING
This means controlling current costs and forecasting future costs. This forecast is based on past experience, future plans and programs, as well as current costs.

You will note that these seven functions can fall under three topics:

Planning) Make a plan Organizing)	Staffing) Directing) Get things done Controlling)	Reporting) Watch it work Budgeting)

PLANNING TO MEET MANAGEMENT GOALS

I. WHAT IS PLANNING?

A. Thinking a job through before new work is done to determine the best way to do it
B. A method of doing something
C. Ways and means for achieving set goals
D. A means of enabling a supervisor to deliver with a minimum of effort, all details involved in coordinating his work

II. WHO SHOULD MAKE PLANS?

Everybody!
All levels of supervision must plan work. (Top management, heads of divisions or bureaus, first line supervisors, and individual employees.) The higher the level, the more planning required.

III. WHAT ARE THE RESULTS OF POOR PLANNING?

A. Failure to meet deadline
B. Low employee morale
C. Lack of job coordination
D. Overtime is frequently necessary
E. Excessive cost, waste of material and manhours

IV. PRINCIPLES OF PLANNING

A. Getting a clear picture of your objectives. What exactly are you trying to accomplish?
B. Plan the whole job, then the parts, in proper sequence.
C. Delegate the planning of details to those responsible for executing them.
D. Make your plan flexible.
E. Coordinate your plan with the plans of others so that the work may be processed with a minimum of delay.
F. Sell your plan before you execute it.
G. Sell your plan to your superior, subordinate, in order to gain maximum participation and coordination.
H. Your plan should take precedence. Use knowledge and skills that others have brought to a similar job.
I. Your plan should take account of future contingencies; allow for future expansion.
J. Plans should include minor details. Leave nothing to chance that can be anticipated.
K. Your plan should be simple and provide standards and controls. Establish quality and quantity standards and set a standard method of doing the job. The controls will indicate whether the job is proceeding according to plan.
L. Consider possible bottlenecks, breakdowns, or other difficulties that are likely to arise.

V. Q. WHAT ARE THE YARDSTICKS BY WHICH PLANNING SHOULD BE MEASURED?

A. Any plan should:

—Clearly state a definite course of action to be followed and goal to be achieved, with consideration for emergencies.
— Be realistic and practical.
— State what's to be done, when it's to be done, where, how, and by whom.
— Establish the most efficient sequence of operating steps so that more is accomplished in less time, with the least effort, and with the best quality results.
— Assure meeting deliveries without delays.
— Establish the standard by which performance is to be judged.

Q. WHAT KINDS OF PLANS DOES EFFECTIVE SUPERVISION REQUIRE?

A. Plans should cover such factors as:

— Manpower: right number of properly trained employees on the job
— Materials: adequate supply of the right materials and supplies
— Machines: full utilization of machines and equipment, with proper maintenance
— Methods: most efficient handling of operations
— Deliveries: making deliveries on time
— Tools: sufficient well-conditioned tools
— Layout: most effective use of space
— Reports: maintaining proper records and reports
— Supervision: planning work for employees and organizing supervisor's own time

MANAGEMENT PRINCIPLES

I. MANAGEMENT

Q. What do we mean by management?

A. Getting work done through others.

Management could also be defined as planning, directing, and controlling the operations of a bureau or division so that all factors will function properly and all persons cooperate efficiently for a common objective.

II. MANAGEMENT PRINCIPLES

A. There should be a hierarchy—wherein authority and responsibility run upward and downward through several levels—with a broad base at the bottom and a single head at the top.

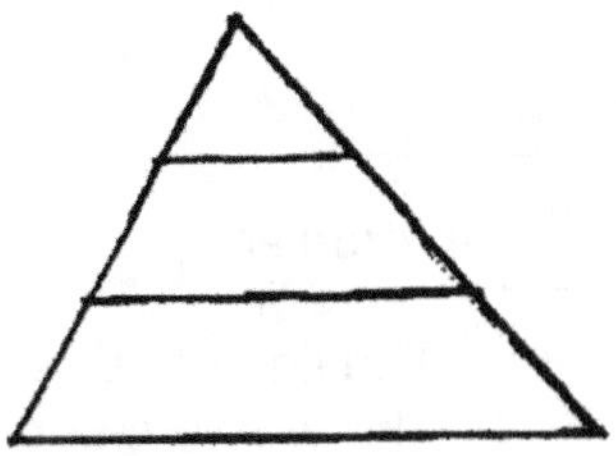

B. Each and every unit or person in the organization should be answerable ultimately to the manager at the apex. In other words, *The buck stops here!*

C. Every necessary function involved in the bureau's objectives is assigned to a unit in that bureau.

D. Responsibilities assigned to a unit are specifically clear-cut and understood.

E. Consistent methods of organizational structure should be applied at each level of the organization.

F. Each member of the bureau from top to bottom knows: to whom he reports and who reports to him.

G. No member of one bureau reports to more than one supervisor. No dual functions.

H. Responsibility for a function is matched by authority necessary to perform that function. Weight of authority.

I. Individuals or units reporting to a supervisor do not exceed the number which can be feasibly and effectively coordinated and directed. Concept of *span of control.*

J. Channels of command (management) are not violated by staff units, although there should be staff services to facilitate and coordinate management functions.

K. Authority and responsibility should be decentralized to units and individuals who are responsible for the actual performance of operations.
Welfare – down to Welfare Centers
Hospitals – down to local hospitals

L. Management should exercise control through attention to policy problems of exceptional performance, rather than through review of routine actions of subordinates.

M. Organizations should never be permitted to grow so elaborate as to hinder work accomplishments.

III. ORGANIZATION STRUCTURE

Types of Organizations
The purest form is a leader and a few followers, such as:

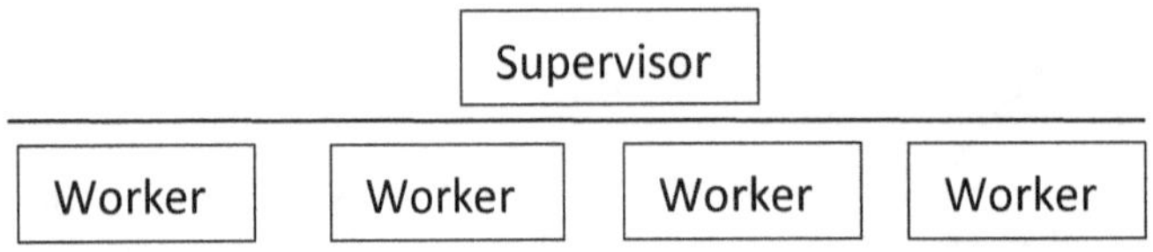

(Refer to organization chart) from supervisor to workers.

The line of authority is direct, The workers know exactly where they stand in relation to their boss, to whom they report for instructions and direction.

Unfortunately, in our present complex society, few organizations are similar to this example of a pure line organization. In this era of specialization, other people are often needed in the simplest of organizations. These specialists are known as staff. The sole purpose for their existence (staff) is to assist, advise, suggest, help or counsel line organizations. Staff has no authority to direct line people—nor do they give them direct instructions.

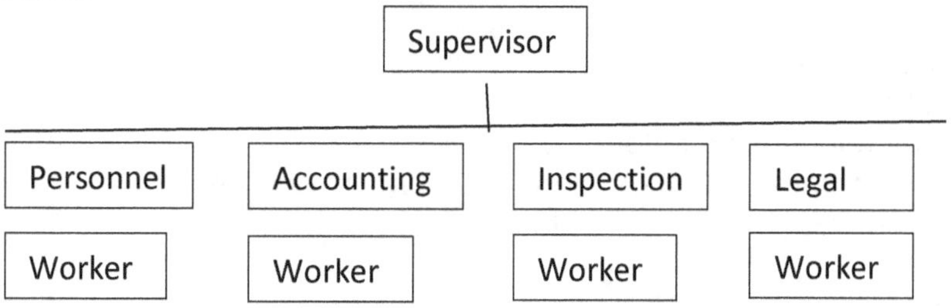

Line Functions
1. Directs
2. Orders
3. Responsibility for carrying out activities from beginning to end
4. Follows chain of command
5. Is identified with what it does
6. Decides when and how to use staff advice
7. Line executes

Staff Functions
1. Advises
2. Persuades and sells
3. Staff studies, reports, recommends but does not carry out
4. May advise across department lines
5. May find its ideas identified with others
6. Has to persuade line to want its advice
7. Staff: Conducts studies and research. Provides advice and instructions in technical matters. Serves as technical specialist to render specific services.

Types and Functions of Organization Charts
An organization chart is a picture of the arrangement and inter-relationship of the subdivisions of an organization.

A. Types of Charts:
   1. Structural: basic relationships only
   2. Functional: includes functions or duties
   3. Personnel: positions, salaries, status, etc.
   4. Process Chart: work performed
   5. Gantt Chart: actual performance against planned
   5. Flow Chart: flow and distribution of work

B. Functions of Charts:
   1. Assist in management planning and control
   2. Indicate duplication of functions
   3. Indicate incorrect stressing of functions
   4. Indicate neglect of important functions
   5. Correct unclear authority
   6. Establish proper span of control

C. Limitations of Charts:
   1. Seldom maintained on current basis
   2. Chart is oversimplified
   3. Human factors cannot adequately be charted

D. Organization Charts should be:
   1. Simple
   2. Symmetrical
   3. Indicate authority
   4. Line and staff relationship differentiated
   5. Chart should be dated and bear signature of approving officer
   6. Chart should be displayed, not hidden

ORGANIZATION

There are four basic principles of organization:

1. Unity of command
2. Span of control
3. Uniformity of assignment
4. Assignment of responsibility and delegation of authority

I. UNITY OF COMMAND

Unity of command means that each person in the organization should receive orders from one, and only one, supervisor. When a person has to take orders from two or more people, (a) the orders may be in conflict and the employee is upset because he does not know which he should obey, or (b) different orders may reach him at the same time and he does not know which he should carry out first.

Equally as bad as having two bosses is the situation where the supervisor is bypassed. Let us suppose you are a supervisor whose boss bypasses you (deals directly with people reporting to you). To the worker, it is the same as having two bosses; but to you, the supervisor, it is equally serious. Bypassing on the part of your boss will undermine your authority, and the people under you will begin looking to your boss for decisions and even for routine orders.

You can prevent bypassing by telling the people you supervise that if anyone tries to give them orders, they should direct that person to you.

II. SPAN OF CONTROL

Span of control on a given level involves:

A. The number of people being supervised
B. The distance
C The time involved in supervising the people. (One supervisor cannot supervise too many workers effectively.)

Span of control means that a supervisor has the right number (not too many and not too few) of subordinates that he can supervise well.

III. UNIFORMITY OF ASSIGNMENT

In assigning work, you as the supervisor should assign to each person jobs that are similar in nature. An employee who is assigned too many different types of jobs will waste time in going from one kind of work to another. It takes time for him to get to top production in one kind of task and, before he does so, he has to start on another.
When you assign work to people, remember that:

A. Job duties should be definite. Make it clear from the beginning what they are to do, how they are to do it, and why they are to do it. Let them know how much they are expected to do and how well they are expected to do it.
B. Check your assignments to be certain that there are no workers with too many unrelated duties, and that no two people have been given overlapping responsibilities. Your aim should be to have every task assigned to a specific person with the work fairly distributed and with each person doing his part.

IV. ASSIGNMENT OF RESPONSIBILITY AND DELEGATION OF AUTHORITY

A supervisor cannot delegate his final responsibility for the work of his department. The experienced supervisor knows that he gets his work done through people. He can't do it all himself. So he must assign the work and the responsibility for the work to his employees. Then they must be given the authority to carry out their responsibilities.

By assigning responsibility and delegating authority to carry out the responsibility, the supervisor builds in his workers initiative, resourcefulness, enthusiasm, and interest in their work. He is treating them as responsible adults. They can find satisfaction in their work, and they will respect the supervisor and be loyal to the supervisor.

PRINCIPLES OF ORGANIZATION

I. DEFINITION

Organization is the method of dividing up the work to provide the best channels for coordinated effort to get the agency's mission accomplished.

II. PURPOSE OF ORGANIZATION

A. To enable each employee within the organization to clearly know his responsibilities and relationships to his fellow employees and to organizational units
B. To avoid conflicts of authority and overlapping of jurisdiction.
C. To ensure teamwork.

III. BASIC CONSIDERATIONS IIN ORGANIZATIONAL PLANNING

A. The basic plans and objectives of the agency should be determined, and the organizational structure should be adapted to carry out effectively such plans and objectives.
B. The organization should be built around the major functions of the agency and not individuals or groups of individuals.

C. The organization should be sufficiently flexible to meet new and changing conditions which may be brought about from within or outside the department.
D. The organizational structure should be as simple as possible and the number of organizational units kept at a minimum.
E. The number of levels of authority should be kept at a minimum. Each additional management level lengthens the chain of authority and responsibility and increases the time for instructions to be distributed to operating levels and for decisions to be obtained from higher authority.
F. The form of organization should permit each executive to exercise maximum initiative within the limits of delegated authority.

IV. BASES FOR ORGANIZATION

A. Purpose (Examples: education, police, sanitation)
B. Process (Examples: accounting, legal, purchasing)
C. Clientele (Examples: welfare, parks, veteran)
D. Geographic (Examples: borough offices, precincts, libraries)

V. ASSIGNMENTS OF FUNCTIONS

A. Every function of the agency should be assigned to a specific organizational unit. Under normal circumstances, no single function should be assigned to more than one organizational unit.
B. There should be no overlapping, duplication, or conflict between organizational elements.
C. Line functions should be separated from staff functions, and proper emphasis should be placed on staff activities.
D. Functions which are closely related or similar should normally be assigned to a single organizational unit.
E. Functions should be properly distributed to promote balance, and to avoid overemphasis of less important functions and underemphasis of more essential functions.

VI. DELEGATION OF AUTHORITY AND RESPONSIBILITY

A. Responsibilities assigned to a specific individual or organizational unit should carry corresponding authority, and all statements of authority or limitations thereof should be as specific as possible.
B. Authority and responsibility for action should be decentralized to organizational units and individuals responsible for actual performance to the greatest extent possible, without relaxing necessary control over policy or the standardization of procedures. Delegation of authority will be consistent with decentralization of responsibility but such delegation will not divest an executive in higher authority of his overall responsibility.
C. The heads of organizational units should concern themselves with important matters and should delegate to the maximum extent details and routines performed in the ordinary course of business.
D. All responsibilities, authorities, and relationships should be stated in simple language to avoid misinterpretation.
E. Each individual or organizational unit charged with a specific responsibility will be held responsible for results.

VII. EMPLOYEE RELATIONSHIPS

A. The employees reporting to one executive should not exceed the number which can be effectively directed and coordinated. The number will depend largely upon the scope and extent of the responsibilities of the subordinates.
B. No person should report to more than one supervisor. Every supervisor should know who reports to him, and every employee should know to whom he reports. Channels of authority and responsibility should not be violated by staff units.
C. Relationships between organizational units within the agency and with outside organizations and associations should be clearly stated and thoroughly understood to avoid misunderstanding.

DELEGATING

I. WHAT IS DELEGATING?
Delegating is assigning a job to an employee, giving him the authority to get that job done, and giving him the responsibility for seeing to it that the job is done.

A. What To Delegate
1. Routine details
2. Jobs which may be necessary and take a lot of time, but do not have to be done by the supervisor personally (preparing reports, attending meetings, etc.)
3. Routine decision-making (making decisions which do not require the supervisor's personal attention)

B. What Not To Delegate
1. Job details which are *executive functions* (setting goals, organizing employees into a good team, analyzing results so as to plan for the future)
2. Disciplinary power (handling grievances, preparing service ratings, reprimands, etc.)
3. Decision-making which involves large numbers of employees or other bureaus and departments
4. Final and complete responsibility for the job done by the unit being supervised

C. Why Delegate?
1. To strengthen the organization by developing a greater number of skilled employees
2. To improve the employee's performance by giving him the chance to learn more about the job, handle some responsibility, and become more interested in getting the job done
3. To improve a supervisor's performance by relieving him of routine jobs and giving him more time for *executive functions* (planning, organizing, controlling, etc.) which cannot be delegated

II. TO WHOM TO DELEGATE
People with abilities not being used. Selection should be based on ability, not on favoritism.

REPORTS

I. DEFINITION
A report is an orderly presentation of factual information directed to a specific reader for a specific purpose

II. PURPOSE
The general purpose of a report is to bring to the reader useful and factual information about a condition or a problem. Some specific purposes of a report may be:

A. To enable the reader to appraise the efficiency or effectiveness of a person or an operation
B. To provide a basis for establishing standards
C. To reflect the results of expenditures of time, effort, and money
D. To provide a basis for developing or altering programs

III. TYPES

A. Information Report: Contains facts arranged in sequence
B. Summary (Examination) Report: Contains facts plus an analysis or discussion of the significance of the facts. Analysis may give advantages and disadvantages or give qualitative and quantitative comparisons
C. Recommendation Report: Contains facts, analysis, and conclusion logically drawn from the facts and analysis, plus a recommendation based upon the facts, analysis, and conclusions

IV. FACTORS TO CONSIDER BEFORE WRITING REPORT

A. <u>Why</u> write the report?: The purpose of the report should be clearly defined.
B. <u>Who</u> will read the report?: What level of language should be used? Will the reader understand professional or technical language?
C. <u>What</u> should be said?: What does the reader need or want to know about the subject?
D. <u>How</u> should it be said?: Should the subject be presented tactfully? Convincingly? In a stimulating manner?

V. PREPARATORY STEPS

A. Assemble the facts: Find out who, why, what, where, when, and how.
B. Organize the facts: Eliminate unnecessary information
C. Prepare an outline: Check for orderliness, logical sequence
D. Prepare a draft: Check for correctness, clearness, completeness, conciseness, and tone
E. Prepare it in final form: Check for grammar, punctuation, appearance

VI. OUTLINE FOR A RECOMMENDATION REPORT

Is the report:
A. Correct in information, grammar, and tone?
B. Clear?
C. Complete?

D. Concise?
E. Timely?
F. Worth its cost?

Will the report accomplish its purpose?

MANAGEMENT CONTROLS

I. CONTROL

What is control? What is controlled? Who controls?

The essence of control is action which adjusts operations to predetermined standards, and its basis is information in the hands of managers. Control is checking to determine whether plans are being observed and suitable progress toward stated objectives is being made, and action is taken, if necessary, to correct deviations.

We have a ready-made model for this concept of control in the automatic systems which are widely used for process control in the chemical land petroleum industries. A process control system works this way. Suppose, for example, it is desired to maintain a constant rate of flow of oil through a pipe at a predetermined or set-point value. A signal, whose strength represents the rate of flow, can be produced in a measuring device and transmitted to a control mechanism. The control mechanism, when it detects any deviation of the actual from the set-point signal, will reposition the value regulating flow rate.

II. BASIS FOR CONTROL

A process control mechanism thus acts to adjust operations to predetermined standards and does so on the basis of information it receives. In a parallel way, information reaching a manager gives him the opportunity for corrective action and is his basis for control. He cannot exercise control without such information, and he cannot do a complete job of managing without controlling.

III. POLICY

What is policy?

Policy is simply a statement of an organization's intention to act in certain ways when specified types of circumstances arise. It represents a general decision, predetermined and expressed as a principle or rule, establishing a normal pattern of conduct for dealing with given types of business events—usually recurrent. A statement is therefore useful in economizing the time of managers and in assisting them to discharge their responsibilities equitably and consistently.

Policy is not a means of control, but policy does generate the need for control.

Adherence to policies is not guaranteed nor can it be taken on faith. It has to be verified. Without verification, there is no basis for control. Policy and procedures, although closely related and interdependent to a certain extent, are not synonymous. A policy may be adopted, for example, to maintain a materials inventory not to exceed one million dollars.

A procedure for inventory control could interpret that policy and convert it into methods for keeping within that limit, with consideration, too, of possible but foreseeable expedient deviation.

IV. PROCEDURE

What is procedure?

A procedure specifically prescribes:

A. What work is to be performed by the various participants
B. Who are the respective participants
C. When and where the various steps in the different processes are to be performed
D. The sequence of operations that will insure uniform handling of recurring transactions
E. The paper that is involved, its origin, transition, and disposition

Necessary appurtenances to a procedure are:

A. Detailed organizational chart
B. Flow charts
C. Exhibits of forms, all presented in close proximity to the text of the procedure

V. BASIS OF CONTROL – INFORMATION IN THE HANDS OF MANAGERS

If the basis of control is information in the hands of managers, then reporting is elevated to a level of very considerable importance.

Types of reporting may include:

A. Special reports and routine reports
B. Written, oral, and graphic reports
C. Staff meetings
D. Conferences
E. Television screens
F. Non-receipt of information, as where management is by exception
G. Any other means whereby information is transmitted to a manager as a basis for control action

FRAMEWORK OF MANAGEMENT

I. ELEMENTS

A. Policy: It has to be verified, controlled.

B. Organization is part of the giving of an assignment. The organizational chart gives to each individual in his title, a first approximation of the nature of his assignment and orients him as being accountable to a certain individual. Organization is not in a true sense a means of control. Control is checking to ascertain whether the assignment is executed as intended and acting on the basis of that information.

C. Budgets perform three functions:
    1. They present the objectives, plans, and programs of the organization in financial terms.

2. They report the progress of actual performance against these predetermined objectives, plans, and programs.
3. Like organizational charts, delegations of authority, procedures, and job descriptions, they define the assignments which have flowed from the Chief Executive. Budgets are a means of control in the respect that they report progress of actual performance against the program. They provide information which enables managers to take action directed toward bringing actual results into conformity with the program.

D. Internal Check provides in practice for the principle that the same person should not have responsibility for all phases of a transaction. This makes it clearly an aspect of organization rather than of control. Internal Check is static, or built-in.

E. Plans, Programs, Objectives
People must know what they are trying to do. Objectives fulfill this need. Without them, people may work industriously and yet, working aimlessly, accomplish little. Plans and Programs complement Objectives, since they propose how and according to what time schedule the objectives are to be reached.

F. Delegations of Authority
Among the ways we have for supplementing the titles and lines of authority of an organizational chart are delegations of authority. Delegations of authority clarify the extent of authority of individuals and in that way serve to define assignments. That they are not means of control is apparent from the very fact that wherever there has been a delegation of authority, the need for control increases. This could hardly be expected to happen if delegations of authority were themselves means of control.

II. MANAGER'S RESPONSIBILITY

Control becomes necessary whenever a manager delegates authority to a subordinate because he cannot delegate and then simply sit back and forget4 about it. A manager's accountability to his own superior has not diminished one whit as a result of delegating part of his authority to a subordinate. The manager must exercise control over actions taken under the authority so delegated. That means checking serves as a basis for possible corrective action.

Objectives, plans, programs, organizational charts, and other elements of the managerial system are not fruitfully regarded as either controls or means of control. They are pre-established standards or models of performance to which operations are adjusted by the exercise of management control. These standards or models of performance are dynamic in character for they are constantly altered, modified, or revised. Policies, organizational set-up, procedures, delegations, etc. are constantly altered but, like objectives and plans, they remain in force until they are either abandoned or revised. All of the elements (or standards or models of performance), objectives, plans, and programs, policies, organization, etc. can be regarded as a *framework of management*.

III. CONTROL TECHNIQUES

Examples of control techniques:
A. Compare against established standards
B. Compare with a similar operation
C. Compare with past operations
D. Compare with predictions of accomplishment

IV. WHERE FORECASTS FIT

Control is after-the-fact while forecasts are before. Forecasts and projections are important for setting objectives and formulating plans.

Information for aiming and planning does not have to be before-the-fact. It may be an after-the-fact analysis proving that a certain policy has been impolitic in its effect on the relation of the company or department with customer, employee, taxpayer, or stockholder; or that a certain plan is no longer practical, or that a certain procedure is unworkable.

The prescription here certainly would not be in control (in these cases, control would simply bring operations into conformity with obsolete standards) but the establishment of new standards, a new policy, a new plan, and a new procedure to be controlled too.

Information is, of course, the basis for all communication in addition to furnishing evidence to management of the need for reconstructing the framework of management.

PROBLEM SOLVING

The accepted concept in modern management for problem solving is the utilization of the following steps:

A. Identify the problem
B. Gather data
C. List possible solutions
D. Test possible solutions
E. Select the best solution
F. Put the solution into actual practice

Occasions might arise where you would have to apply the second step of gathering data before completing the first step.

You might also find that it will be necessary to work on several steps at the same time.

I. IDENTIFY THE PROBLEM

Your first step is to define as precisely as possible the problem to be solved. While this may sound easy, it is often the most difficult part of the process.

It has been said of problem solving that you are halfway to the solution when you can write out a clear statement of the problem itself.

Our job now is to get below the surface manifestations of the trouble and pinpoint the problem. This is usually accomplished by a logical analysis, by going from the general to the particular; from the obvious to the not-so-obvious cause.

Let us say that production is behind schedule. WHY? Absenteeism is high. Now, is absenteeism the basic problem to be tackled, or is it merely a symptom of low morale among the workforce? Under these circumstances, you may decide that production is not the problem; the problem is *employee morale*.

In trying to define the problem, remember there is seldom one simple reason why production is lagging, or reports are late, etc.

Analysis usually leads to the discovery that an apparent problem is really made up of several subproblems which must be attacked separately.

Another way is to limit the problem, and thereby ease the task of finding a solution, and concentrate on the elements which are within the scope of your control.

When you have gone this far, write out a tentative statement of the problem to be solved.

II. GATHER DATA

In the second step, you must set out to collect all the information that might have a bearing on the problem. Do not settle for an assumption when reasonable fact and figures are available.

If you merely go through the motions of problem-solving, you will probably shortcut the information-gathering step. Therefore, do not stack the evidence by confining your research to your own preconceived ideas.

As you collect facts, organize them in some form that helps you make sense of them and spot possible relationships between them. For example, plotting cost per unit figures on a graph can be more meaningful than a long column of figures.

Evaluate each item as you go along. Is the source material absolutely, reliable, probably reliable, or not to be trusted.

One of the best methods for gathering data is to go out and look the situation over carefully. Talk to the people on the job who are most affected by this problem.

Always keep in mind that a primary source is usually better than a secondary source of information.

III. LIST POSSIBLE SOLUTIONS

This is the creative thinking step of problem solving. This is a good time to bring into play whatever techniques of group dynamics the agency or bureau might have developed for a joint attack on problems.

Now the important thing for you to do is: Keep an open mind. Let your imagination roam freely over the facts you have collected. Jot down every possible solution that occurs to you. Resist the temptation to evaluate various proposals as you go along. List seemingly absurd ideas along with more plausible ones. The more possibilities you list during this step, the less risk you will run of settling for merely a workable, rather than the best, solution.

Keep studying the data as long as there seems to be any chance of deriving additional ideas, solutions, explanations, or patterns from it.

IV. TEST POSSIBLE SOLUTIONS

Now you begin to evaluate the possible solutions. Take pains to be objective. Up to this point, you have suspended judgment but you might be tempted to select a solution you secretly favored all along and proclaim it as the best of the lot.

The secret of objectivity in this phase is to test the possible solutions separately, measuring each against a common yardstick. To make this yardstick try to enumerate as many specific criteria as you can think of. Criteria are best phrased as questions which you ask of each possible solution. They can be drawn from these general categories:

Suitability – Will this solution do the job?
Will it solve the problem completely or partially?
Is it a permanent or a stopgap solution?

Feasibility - Will this plan work in actual practice?
Can we afford this approach?
How much will it cost?

Acceptability - Will the boss go along with the changes required in the plan?
Are we trying to drive a tack with a sledge hammer?

V. SELECT THE BEST SOLUTION

This is the area of executive decision.

Occasionally, one clearly superior solution will stand out at the conclusion of the testing process. But often it is not that simple. You may find that no one solution has come through all the tests with flying colors.

You may also find that a proposal, which flunked miserably on one of the essential tests, racked up a very high score on others.

The best solution frequently will turn out to be a combination.

Try to arrange a marriage that will bring together the strong points of one possible solution with the particular virtues of another. The more skill and imagination that you apply, the greater is the likelihood that you will come out with a solution that is not merely adequate and workable, but is the best possible under the circumstances.

VI. PUT THE SOLUTION INTO ACTUAL PRACTICE

As every executive knows, a plan which works perfectly on paper may develop all sorts of bugs when put into actual practice.

Problem-solving does not stop with selecting the solution which looks best in theory. The next step is to put the chosen solution into action and watch the results. The results may point towards modifications.

If the problem disappears when you put your solution into effect, you know you have the right solution.

If it does not disappear, even after you have adjusted your plan to cover unforeseen difficulties that turned up in practice, work your way back through the problem-solving solutions.

Would one of them have worked better?
Did you overlook some vital piece of data which would have given you a different slant on the whole situation? Did you apply all necessary criteria in testing solutions? If no light dawns after this much rechecking, it is a pretty good bet that you defined the problem incorrectly in the first place.

You came up with the wrong solution because you tackled the wrong problem.

Thus, step six may become step one of a new problem-solving cycle.

COMMUNICATION

I. WHAT IS COMMUNICATION?
We communicate through writing, speaking, action, or inaction. In speaking to people face-to-face, there is opportunity to judge reactions and to adjust the message. This makes the supervisory chain one of the most, and in many instances the most, important channels of communication.

In an organization, communication means keeping employees informed about the organization's objectives, policies, problems, and progress. Communication is the free interchange of information, ideas, and desirable attitudes between and among employees and between employees and management.

II. WHY IS COMMUNICATION NEEDED?

A. People have certain social needs
B. Good communication is essential in meeting those social needs
C. While people have similar basic needs, at the same time they differ from each other
D. Communication must be adapted to these individual differences

An employee cannot do his best work unless he knows why he is doing it. If he has the feeling that he is being kept in the dark about what is going on, his enthusiasm and productivity suffer.

Effective communication is needed in an organization so that employees will understand what the organization is trying to accomplish; and how the work of one unit contributes to or affects the work of other units in the organization and other organizations.

III. HOW IS COMMUNICATION ACHIEVED?

Communication flows downward, upward, sideways.

A. Communication may come from top management down to employees. This is downward communication.

Some means of downward communication are:
1. Training (orientation, job instruction, supervision, public relations, etc.)
2. Conferences
3. Staff meetings
4. Policy statements
5. Bulletins
6. Newsletters
7. Memoranda
8. Circulation of important letters

In downward communication, it is important that employees be informed in advance of changes that will affect them.

B. Communications should also be developed so that the ideas, suggestions, and knowledge of employees will flow upward to top management.

Some means of upward communication are:
1. Personal discussion conferences
2. Committees
3. Memoranda
4. Employees suggestion program
5. Questionnaires to be filled in giving comments and suggestions about proposed actions that will affect field operations.

Upward communication requires that management be willing to listen, to accept, and to make changes when good ideas are present. Upward communication succeeds when there is no fear of punishment for speaking out or lack of interest at the top. Employees will share their knowledge and ideas with management when interest is shown and recognition is given.

C. The advantages of downward communication:
1. It enables the passing down of orders, policies, and plans necessary to the continued operation of the station.
2. By making information available, it diminishes the fears and suspicions which result from misinformation and misunderstanding.
3. It fosters the pride people want to have in their work when they are told of good work.
4. It improves the morale and stature of the individual to be *in the know*.

5. It helps employees to understand, accept, and cooperate with changes when they know about them in advance.

D. The advantages of upward communication:
   1. It enables the passing upward of information, attitudes, and feelings.
   2. It makes it easier to find out how ready people are to receive downward communication.
   3. It reveals the degree to which the downward communication is understood and accepted.
   4. It helps to satisfy the basic social needs.
   5. It stimulates employees to participate in the operation of their organization.
   6. It encourage employees to contribute ideas for improving the efficiency and economy of operations.
   7. It helps to solve problem situations before they reach the explosion point.

IV. WHY DOES COMMUNICATION FAIL?

A. The technical difficulties of conveying information clearly
B. The emotional content of communication which prevents complete transmission
C. The fact that there is a difference between what management needs to say, what it wants to day, and what it does say
D. The fact that there is a difference between what employees would like to say, what they think is profitable or safe to say, and what they do say

V. HOW TO IMPROVE COMMUNICATION

As a supervisor, you are a key figure in communication. To improve as a communicator, you should:

A. Know: Knowing your subordinates will help you to recognize and work with individual differences.
B. Like: If you like those who work for you and those for whom you work, this will foster the kind of friendly, warm, work atmosphere that will facilitate communication.
C. Trust: Showing a sincere desire to communicate will help to develop the mutual trust and confidence which are essential to the free flow of communication.
D. Tell: Tell your subordinates and superiors *what's doing*. Tell your subordinates *why* as well as *how*.
E. Listen: By listening, you help others to talk and you create good listeners. Don't forget that listening implies action.
F. Stimulate: Communication has to be stimulated and encouraged. Be receptive to ideas and suggestions and motivate your people so that each member of the team identifies himself with the job at hand.
G. Consult: The most effective way of consulting is to let your people participate, insofar as possible, in developing determinations which affect them or their work.

VI. HOW TO DETERMINE WHETHER YOU ARE GETTING ACROSS

A. Check to see that communication is received and understood
B. Judge this understanding by actions rather than words
C. Adapt or vary communication, when necessary
D. Remember that good communication cannot cure all problems

VII. THE KEY ATTITUDE

Try to see things from the other person's point of view. By doing this, you help to develop the permissive atmosphere and the shared confidence and understanding which are essential to effective two-way communication.

Communication is a two-way process:

A. The basic purpose of any communication is to get action.
B. The only way to get action is through acceptance.
C. In order to get acceptance, communication must be humanly satisfying as well as technically efficient.

HOW ORDERS AND INSTRUCTIONS SHOULD BE GIVEN

I. CHARACTERISTICS OF GOOD ORDERS AND INSTRUCTIONS

A. Clear
Orders should be definite as to
—What is to be done
—Who is to do it
—When it is to be done
—Where it is to be done
—How it is to be done

B. Concise
Avoid wordiness. Orders should be brief and to the point.

C. Timely
Instructions and orders should be sent out at the proper time and not too long in advance of expected performance.

D. Possibility of Performance
Orders should be feasible:
1. Investigate before giving orders
2. Consult those who are to carry out instructions before formulating and issuing them

E. Properly Directed
Give the orders to the people concerned. Do not send orders to people who are not concerned. People who continually receive instructions that are not applicable to them get in the habit of neglecting instructions generally.

F. Reviewed Before Issuance
Orders should be reviewed before issuance:
1. Test them by putting yourself in the position of the recipient
2. If they involve new procedures, have the persons who are to do the work review them for suggestions.

G. Reviewed After Issuance
Persons who receive orders should be allowed to raise questions and to point out unforeseen consequences of orders.

H. Coordinated
Orders should be coordinated so that work runs smoothly.

I. Courteous
Make a request rather than a demand. There is no need to continually call attention to the fact that you are the boss.

J. Recognizable as an Order
Be sure that the order is recognizable as such.

K. Complete
Be sure recipient has knowledge and experience sufficient to carry out order. Give illustrations and examples.

A DEPARTMENTAL PERSONNEL OFFICE IS RESPONSIBLE FOR THE FOLLOWING FUNCTIONS

1. Policy
2. Personnel Programs
3. Recruitment and Placement
4. Position Classification
5. Salary and Wage Administration
6. Employee performance Standards and Evaluation
7. Employee Relations
8. Disciplinary Actions and Separations
9. Health and Safety
10. Staff Training and Development
11. Personnel Records, Procedures, and Reports
12. Employee Services
13. Personnel Research

SUPERVISION

I. LEADERSHIP

All leadership is based essentially on authority. This comes from two sources: It is received from higher management or it is earned by the supervisor through his methods of supervision. Although effective leadership has always depended upon the leader's using his authority in such a way as to appeal successfully to the motives of the people supervised, the conditions for making this appeal are continually changing. The key to today's problem of leadership is flexibility and resourcefulness on the part of the leader in meeting changes in conditions as they occur.

Three basic approaches to leadership are generally recognized:

A. The Authoritarian Approach
   1. The methods and techniques used in this approach emphasize the *I* in leadership and depend primarily on the formal authority of the leader. This authority is sometimes exercised in a hardboiled manner and sometimes in a benevolent

manner, but in either case the dominating role of the leader is reflected in the thinking, planning, and decisions of the group.

2. Group results are to a large degree dependent on close supervision by the leader. Usually, the individuals in the group will not show a high degree of initiative or acceptance of responsibility and their capacity to grow and develop probably will not be fully utilized. The group may react with resentment or submission, depending upon the manner and skill of the leader in using his authority.
3. This approach develops as a natural outgrowth of the authority that goes with the leader's job and his feeling of sole responsibility for getting the job done. It is relatively easy to use and does not require must resourcefulness.
4. The use of this approach is effective in times of emergencies, in meeting close deadline as a final resort, in settling some issues, in disciplinary matters, and with dependent individuals and groups.

B. The Laissez-Faire or Let 'em Alone Approach

1. This approach generally is characterized by an avoidance of leadership responsibility by the leader. The activities of the group depend largely on the choice of its members rather than the leader.
2. Group results probably will be poor. Generally, there will be disagreements over petty things, bickering, and confusion. Except for a few aggressive people, individuals will not show much initiative and growth and development will be retarded. There may be a tendency for informal leaders to take over leadership of the group.
3. This approach frequently results from the leader's dislike of responsibility, from his lack of confidence, from failure of other methods to work, from disappointment or criticism. It is usually the easiest of the three to use and requires both understanding and resourcefulness on the part of the leader.
4. This approach is occasionally useful and effective, particularly in forcing dependent individuals or groups to rely on themselves, to give someone a chance to save face by clearing his own difficulties, or when action should be delayed temporarily for good cause.

C. The Democratic Approach

1. The methods and techniques used in this approach emphasize the *we* in leadership and build up the responsibility of the group to attain its objectives. Reliance is placed largely on the earned authority of the leader.
2. Group results are likely to be good because most of the job motives of the people will be satisfied. Cooperation and teamwork, initiative, acceptance of responsibility, and the individual's capacity for growth probably will show a high degree of development.
3. This approach grows out of a desire or necessity of the leader to find ways to appeal effectively to the motivation of his group. It is the best approach to build up inside the person a strong desire to cooperate and apply himself to the job. It is the most difficult to develop, and requires both understanding and resourcefulness on the part of the leader.
4. The value of this approach increases over a long period where sustained efficiency and development of people are important. It may not be fully effective in all situations, however, particularly when there is not sufficient time to use it properly or where quick decisions must be made.

All three approaches are used by most leaders and have a place in supervising people. The extent of their use varies with individual leaders, with some using one approach predominantly. The leader who uses these three approaches, and varies their use with time and circumstance, is probably the most effective. Leadership which is used predominantly with a democratic approach requires more resourcefulness on the part of the leader but offers the greatest possibilities in terms of teamwork and cooperation.

The one best way of developing democratic leadership is to provide a real sense of participation on the part of the group, since this satisfies most of the chief job motives. Although there are many ways of providing participation, consulting as frequently as possible with individuals and groups on things that affect them seems to offer the most in building cooperation and responsibility. Consultation takes different forms, but it is most constructive when people feel they are actually helping in finding the answers to the problems on the job.

There are some requirements of leaders in respect to human relations which should be considered in their selection and development. Generally, the leader should be interested in working with other people, emotionally stable, self-confident, and sensitive to the reactions of others. In addition, his viewpoint should be one of getting the job done through people who work cooperatively in response to his leadership. He should have a knowledge of individual and group behavior, but, most important of all, he should work to combine all of these requirements into a definite, practical skill in leadership.

II. NINE POINTS OF CONTRAST BETWEEN *BOSS* AND *LEADER*

A. The boss drives his men; the leader coaches them.
B. The boss depends on authority; the leader on good will.
C. The boss inspires fear; the leader inspires enthusiasm.
D. The boss says I; the leader says *We*.
E. The boss says *Get here on time*; the leader gets there ahead of time.
F. The boss fixes the blame for the breakdown; the leader fixes the breakdown.
G. The boss knows how it is done; the leader shows how.
H. The boss makes work a drudgery; the leader makes work a game.
I. The boss says *Go*; the leader says *Let's go*.

EMPLOYEE MORALE

Employee morale is the way employees feel about each other, the organization or unit in which they work, and the work they perform.

I. SOME WAYS TO DEVELOP AND MAINTAIN GOOD EMPLYEE MORALE

A. Give adequate credit and praise when due.
B. Recognize importance of all jobs and equalize load with proper assignments, always giving consideration to personality differences and abilities.
C. Welcome suggestions and do not have an *all-wise* attitude. Request employees' assistance in solving problems and use assistants when conducting group meetings on certain subjects.
D. Properly assign responsibilities and give adequate authority for fulfillment of such assignments.

E. Keep employees informed about matters that affect them.
F. Criticize and reprimand employees privately.
G. Be accessible and willing to listen.
H. Be fair.
I. Be alert to detect training possibilities so that you will not miss an opportunity to help each employee do a better job, and if possible with less effort on his part.
J. Set a good example.
K. Apply the golden rule.

II. SOME INDICATIONS OF GOOD MORALE

A. Good quality of work
B. Good quantity
C. Good attitude of employees
D. Good discipline
E. Teamwork
F. Good attendance
G. Employee participation

MOTIVATION

DRIVES

A drive, stated simply, is a desire or force which causes a person to do or say certain things. These are some of the most usual drives and some of their identifying characteristics recognizable in people motivated by such drives:

A. Security (desire to provide for the future)
Always on time for work
Works for the same employer for many years
Never takes unnecessary chances
Seldom resists doing what he is told

B. Recognition (desire to be rewarded for accomplishment)
Likes to be asked for his opinion
Becomes very disturbed when he makes a mistake
Does things to attract attention
Likes to see his name in print

C. Position (desire to hold certain status in relation to others)
Boasts about important people he knows
Wants to be known as a key man
Likes titles
Demands respect
Belongs to clubs, for prestige

D. Accomplishment (desire to get things done)
Complains when things are held up
Likes to do things that have tangible results
Never lies down on the job
Is proud of turning out good work

E. Companionship (desire to associate with other people)
Likes to work with others
Tells stories and jokes
Indulges in horseplay
Finds excuses to talk to others on the job

F. Possession (desire to collect and hoard objects)
Likes to collect things
Puts his name on things belonging to him
Insists on the same location

Supervisors may find that identifying the drives of employees is a helpful step toward motivating them to self-improvement and better job performance. For example: An employee's job performance is below average. His supervisor, having previously determined that the employee is motivated by a drive for security, suggests that taking training courses will help the employee to improve, advance, and earn more money. Since earning more money can be a step toward greater security, the employee's drive for security would motivate him to take the training suggested by the supervisor. In essence, this is the process of charting an employee's future course by using his motivating drives to positive advantage.

EMPLOYEE PARTICIPATION

I. WHAT IS PARTICIPATION

Employee participation is the employee's giving freely of his time, skill, and knowledge to an extent which cannot be obtained by demand.

II. WHY IS IT IMPORTANT?

The supervisor's responsibility is to get the job done through people. A good supervisor gets the job done through people who work willingly and well. The participation of employees is important because:

A. Employees develop a greater sense of responsibility when they share in working out operating plans and goals.
B. Participation provides greater opportunity and stimulation for employees to learn, and to develop their ability.
C. Participation sometimes provides better solutions to problems because such solutions may combine the experience and knowledge of interested employees who want the solutions to work.
D. An employee or group may offer a solution which the supervisor might hesitate to make for fear of demanding too much.

E. Since the group wants to make the solution work, they exert pressure in a constructive way on each other.
F. Participation usually results in reducing the need for close supervision.

II. HOW MAY SUPERVISORS OBTAIN IT?

Participation is encouraged when employees feel that they share some responsibility for the work and that their ideas are sincerely wanted and valued. Some ways of obtaining employee participation are:

A. Conduct orientation programs for new employees to inform them about the organization and their rights and responsibilities as employees.
B. Explain the aims and objectives of the agency. On a continuing basis, be sure that the employees know what these aims and objectives are.
C. Share job successes and responsibilities and give credit for success.
D. Consult with employees, both as individuals and in groups, about things that affect them.
E. Encourage suggestions for job improvements. Help employees to develop good suggestions. The suggestions can bring them recognition. The city's suggestion program offers additional encouragement through cash awards.

The supervisor who encourages employee participation is not surrendering his authority. He must still make decisions and initiate action, and he must continue to be ultimately responsible for the work of those he supervises. But, through employee participation, he is helping his group to develop greater ability and a sense of responsibility while getting the job done faster and better.

STEPS IN HANDLING A GRIEVANCE

1. Get the Facts
   a. Listen sympathetically
   b. Let him talk himself out
   c. Get his story straight
   d. Get his point of view
   e. Don't argue with him
   f. Give him plenty of time
   g. Conduct the interview privately
   h. Don't try to shift the blame or pass the buck

2. Consider the Facts
   a. Consider the employee's viewpoint
   b. How will the decision affect similar cases
   c. Consider each decision as a possible precedent
   d. Avoid snap judgments—don't jump to conclusions

3. Make or Get a Decision
   a. Frame an effective counter-proposal
   b. Make sure it is fair to all
   c. Have confidence in your judgment
   d. Be sure you can substantiate your decision

4. Notify the Employee of Your Decision
Be sure he is told; try to convince him that the decision is fair and just.

5. Take Action When Needed and If Within Your Authority
Otherwise, tell employee that the matter will be called to the attention of the proper person or that nothing can be done, and why it cannot.

6. Follow through to see that the desired result is achieved.

7. Record key facts concerning the complaint and the action taken.

8. Leave the way open to him to appeal your decision to a higher authority.

9. Report all grievances to your superior, whether they are appealed or not.

DISCIPLINE

Discipline is training that develops self-control, orderly conduct, and efficiency.

To discipline does not necessarily mean to punish.

To discipline does mean to train, to regulate, and to govern conduct.

I. THE DISCIPLINARY INTERVIEW

Most employees sincerely want to do what is expected of them. In other words, they are self-disciplined. Some employees, however, fail to observe established rules and standards, and disciplinary action by the supervisor is required.

The primary purpose of disciplinary action is to improve conduct without creating dissatisfaction, bitterness, or resentment in the process.

Constructive disciplinary action is more concerned with causes and explanations of breaches of conduct than with punishment. The disciplinary interview is held to get at the causes of apparent misbehavior and to motivate better performance in the future.

It is important that the interview be kept on an impersonal a basis as possible. If the supervisor lets the interview descend to the plane of an argument, it loses its effectiveness.

II. PLANNING THE INTERVIEW

Get all pertinent facts concerning the situation so that you can talk in specific terms to the employee.

Review the employee's record, appraisal ratings, etc.

Consider what you know about the temperament of the employee. Consider your attitude toward the employee. Remember that the primary requisite of disciplinary action is fairness.

Don't enter upon the interview when angry.

Schedule the interview for a place which is private and out of hearing of others.

III. CONDUCTING THE INTERVIEW

A. Make an effort to establish accord.
B. Question the employee about the apparent breach of discipline. Be sure that the question is not so worded as to be itself an accusation.
C. Give the employee a chance to tell his side of the story. Give him ample opportunity to talk.
D. Use understanding—listening except where it is necessary to ask a question or to point out some details of which the employee may not be aware. If the employee misrepresents facts, make a plain, accurate statement of the facts, but don't argue and don't engage in personal controversy.
E. Listen and try to understand the reasons for the employee's (mis)conduct. First of all, don't assume that there has been a breach of discipline. Evaluate the employee's reasons for his conduct in the light of his opinions and feelings concerning the consistency and reasonableness of the standards which he was expected to follow. Has the supervisor done his part in explaining the reasons for the rule? Was the employee's behavior unintentional or deliberate? Does he think he had real reasons for his actions? What new facts is he telling? Do the facts justify his actions? What causes, other than those mentioned, could have stimulated the behavior?
F. After listening to the employee's version of the situation, and if censure of his actions is warranted, the supervisor should proceed with whatever criticism is justified. Emphasis should be placed on future improvement rather than exclusively on the employee's failure to measure up to expected standards of job conduct.
G. Fit the criticism to the individual. With one employee, a word of correction may be all that is required.
H. Attempt to distinguish between unintentional error and deliberate misbehavior. An error due to ignorance requires training and not censure.
I. Administer criticism in a controlled, even tone of voice, never in anger. Make it clear that you are acting as an agent of the department. In general, criticism should refer to the job or the employee's actions and not to the person. Criticism of the employee's work is not an attack on the individual.
J. Be sure the interview does not destroy the employee's self-confidence. Mention his good qualities and assure him that you feel confident that he can improve his performance.
K. Wherever possible, before the employee leaves the interview, satisfy him that the incident is closed, that nothing more will be said on the subject unless the offense is repeated.

TECHNIQUES OF DECISION MAKING

CONTENTS

TECHNIQUES OF DECISION MAKING

INSTRUCTIONAL OBJECTIVES

1. Ability to define decision making.
2. Ability to learn the decision-making formula.
3. Ability to learn how to state problems simply and accurately.
4. Ability to determine the difference between a symptom and a cause.
5. Ability to determine which facts are most important to a decision.
6. Ability to be able to qualify information according to importance and subject classification.
7. Ability to learn to identify two or more alternative solutions for a problem.
8. Ability to develop an openness to creative ideas.
9. Ability to learn to weigh the consequences of alternative decisions.
10. Ability to select and justify the most appropriate decision.

CONTENT

<u>INTRODUCTION</u>

Every person, each day, is faced by numerous situations which require the making of many decisions throughout the course of the day. It is necessary to answer such questions as: *When do I get up in the morning? What clothes will I wear? What will I have for breakfast? Which route will I take to school?*

Working in the field of public service, an individual is constantly faced with a series of situations which require him to take some particular course of action. Many such actions may not require special decision making on his part, because his particular organization has provided ways for him to make these decisions rather automatically. For example, there are department policies, and standard ways of performing certain jobs. A person also has his own past experiences of success which enable him to easily make certain decisions for such things as: the hours he should work, his rate of pay, and the required forms which must be completed for certain kinds of activities. All of these things are handled rather automatically on the job, because people have methods of handling certain things in certain ways. These become habit. They fit within a regular pattern.

There are many situations faced by a decision maker where the consequences of his action are so minor that it doesn't really matter which way he decides to solve a given problem as long as it is resolved: for example, what pencil to choose; the color of the paper on a final report; the diverting of automobiles during a traffic jam.

However, there are also other situations where the way a manager or supervisor solves a problem has great impact on an organization. Sometimes a person doesn't have a chance to actually know what is right and what is wrong. Judgment might have no well established basis. The opportunity to select between two alternatives of equal value does not exist. The situation is not clearcut. It requires thought and careful judgment; it has far-reaching consequences on the organization-affecting the quality of service, costs, schedules, the relationships between people in a working unit. Appropriate action must be taken in such assorted areas as overtime, employee dismissal, grievances, types of equipment to purchase, ways to reduce waste. The effectiveness and efficiency of the decision-making process of one individual can have far-reaching impact on a public-service organization.

Good decisions allow individuals to control and monitor their operations. Bad ones can cause worse problems and hinder the effectiveness of an organization. Things just don't happen by chance. They are made to happen. They are arranged. They can quite often be developed over a period of time which has been required by the nature of the problem or activity.

1. <u>WHAT IS DECISION MAKING?</u>

Decision making involves a conscious choice or selection of one behavior alternative from a group of two or more behavior alternatives.

Thus, there are two basic elements in a decision-making process: one, the matter of conscious choice, and the other of alternatives. *To decide, then, really means to cut off, to come to a conclusion, to end.*

2. <u>*A FORMULA FOR DECISION MAKING*</u>

Decision-making is a skill that can be developed. One way in which it can be developed is through a formula, a procedure which provides a formal process or system involving the basic rules of decision-making. There are no born decision makers, but some people appear to act very efficiently on the basis of hunches. These people may never be seen with charts and graphs, or performing a lot of analytical tasks. However, they've probably developed their own way of sifting facts and of solving problems. Good decision makers usually know their personnel; have prior experience; they can put together difficult possibilities quickly. They have their own personal *formulas* of decision making.

An effective technique to help make decisions is through the aid of a formula –a kind of check-off list to help find answers to difficult situations, to resolve problems, to handle unique situations. Such a formula enables one to take advantage of his past experiences, to see the whole picture, and to utilize all the facts he can find which are applicable to the solution.

A decision-making formula worthy of our consideration has six steps:

- *Isolate* - State the apparent problem or situation with which you plan to deal.
- *Analyze* - Gather the facts.
- *Diagnose* - Organize and interpret the facts.
- *Prescribe procedures* - State the real problem or situation.
- *Implement procedures* - Develop alternative solutions.
- *Evaluate* - Select the most appropriate alternative. Decide.

We will consider each of these steps separately. However, it should be kept in mind that these separate steps are really all related and part of the whole process of decision making.

A. *Isolate the Problem*. A problem can be a situation, question, matter, or person that is perplexing or difficult, that obstructs the way to achieving a goal or objective.

Almost everyone has problems: students have study problems when they don't know answers to test questions; people have money problems when they can't pay all of their bills. Individuals have problems with people who are unfriendly; problems with their girlfriends or boyfriends; growth problems; health problems; psychological problems.

There are professionals and specialists to whom people can go with their problems. A person takes his malfunctioning car to a mechanic, he calls on the plumber to fix leaky pipes, contacts the doctor when he doesn't feel well. These specialists are skilled problem solvers in a particular area. They have had special training and experience. They may even have had to pass examinations to obtain certificates or licenses.

In decision making, one must recognize problems as well as symptoms of problems. It is particularly important to be able to separate symptoms from causes.

What is the Real Problem? Problems are often presented in very broad terms: "Gee, John, they've really fouled up in accounting. Go straighten them out." "Boy, do we have a morale problem." "We have to introduce that new system right away." "Those two managers just don't get along."

Consider the question of morale, for example. Is morale really the problem, or is it more accurately the symptom of another problem? Chances are that it is a symptom of a problem rather than the real problem itself. The problem situation might be poor organizational structure, bad working conditions, an unfriendly supervisor, unfair treatment, or a number of other difficulties.

To help in determining what is a symptom and what is a cause, several questions must be asked:

- *"How else might the problem be stated?"* The placement of accountants in one isolated department, without the opportunity to discuss actual income and outgo with supervisors, has given us unrealistic budget figures.

  The lack of adding machines, a broken calculator, dim light, uncomfortable room temperatures, and individual working spaces has caused a greater number of absences.

  The accounting manager has openly criticized senior staff members in front of their fellow workers.

  The department secretaries were all forced to work overtime for staying five minutes past their lunch hours.

- *"What else is involved?"*

  If there are no communications between accountants and supervisors, neither group will know the reasons behind the requests or needs of the others.

  There has been talk about a computer eliminating some of the accounting jobs.

  The senior accountants have been slow to pick up the new accounting procedures.

  This is the tenth time this month that the financial unit has been unable to take care of the people in line because the secretaries were not here.

- *"Are there similar problems in other departments?"*

  The people in supplies have been ordering the wrong equipment.

  There have been layoffs in several departments.

  Several department managers are competing for the job of assistant director of our organization.

  None of the other departments have problems with secretaries.

- *"Is this a problem or a symptom?"*

  The real problem is that the accountants have not been properly informed of the organizational structure, and thus have very poor understanding of the departments which comprise the organization.

  Another organization nearby has announced opportunities for accountants at higher pay, and in new offices.

  The accounting manager and his senior staff do not plan departmental modifications together.

  Only one of the secretaries has a watch and it is five minutes slow. They play bridge at lunch time several days each month.

- *"How do others perceive the problem?"*

  Talk to all the accountants and managers individually.

  Talk to personnel about accounting re-classification.

  Interview the senior staff.

Visit with the secretaries.

<u>What are the Problems? What are the Symptoms?</u> If your automobile won't start, it might not be because it's old, the engine is dirty, or your windshield wipers don't work the car may be out of gas. It might, however, be time to give it some other attention, too. If you can recognize the symptoms, you can avoid a lot of problems.

B. <u>Analyze the Facts.</u> When the problem is recognized, then all the facts required for a successful decision can, and should be accumulated. Too often, people think they have all the facts, but they don't. It's like trying to put together a jigsaw puzzle, and recognizing, after many frustrating hours, that six pieces are missing.

Frequently, the decision maker feels that because he is in a particular situation, he knows it better than anyone else can know it. The issue may, therefore, be somewhat clouded. This cloudiness may prevent him from seeing what is actually there.

How many times have individuals had to make a decision and found that they didn't have the right facts or sufficient quantities of facts to insure a good decision? Both the quality and effectiveness of most decisions can be seriously reduced without good facts.

When gathering facts, one should write them down, and gather them into one comprehensive list. The decision maker can then visualize them all at the same time, and is much less likely to overlook or forget any of them. In dealing with large amounts of information, he can grade sub-topics and keep track of them in a systematic way.

How many facts should be gathered? The number usually depends on the nature and complexity of the situation.

Basically it means that the amount of information accumulated depends upon such factors as:

- The amount of time available.
- Is it an emergency situation or not?
- The seriousness of the situation.
- The availability of information, etc.

Where are the Needed Facts Obtained?

- First, he might turn to available records. He usually has financial records, personal records, records of transactions, and records of activities.
- Second, he may have references: newspapers, journals, old letters, the like.
- Third, and very importantly, he has other people, or he has a staff. There is a great deal of expertise within most public-service organizations: specialists in economics, human relations, law, health, safety, and other areas; all responsive to the request of the decision-maker. An outside expert, or consultant, may be required in difficult situations.
- Finally, look at other organizational units which have been confronted with similar problems. Quite often, through investigation, the decision-maker finds that precedents have been set which he may have to follow. In law, for example, he may have to base a decis.ion on the verdict of a case held on the same issue, long ago in a distant place.

Sources of information are unlimited. It takes a great deal of initiative to uncover them.

How should the facts be obtained? Here again, there are questions we must ask ourselves:

- What kinds of facts are available?
- What information is available?
- Is there enough?

- Is help needed, and where can it be obtained?

- Who else might have the information needed?

Going back to the morale problem, which was found to be the result of a basic lack of communication between accountants and departmental managers, how might the decision-maker proceed?

In gathering the facts, he would have to obtain both the accountant's records and the manager's records. The decision-maker might call upon organizations of similar size and activity, to see how they handle difficulties of this nature. He might talk to one or more senior accountants in a large public accounting firm or contact the governmental auditors. He might even write letters to colleagues seeking their advice.

The decision-maker might hold a meeting of selected members of his staff, or assign a task force of accountants and managers to look into the matter.

As he begins to gather his facts, the decision-maker will discover that other information is required. Additionally, he will uncover sources of other facts. The quality of the facts he gathers ultimately affects the quality of his decisions. The better the data, the better the opportunity to make a good decision.

C. Organizing the Facts. Once the facts have been collected, it becomes very important that they be organized to help the decision-maker interpret what they really mean. To do this, it's helpful to set them up in categories -- to pull like items together.

This procedure helps people to know whether certain facts are more important than others, and thus deserve special consideration.

Grouping the Facts. There are several categories into which information can be grouped, such as: cost, time, past precedent, procedures, leadership, quality, and productivity:

Cost. In cost considerations, one must look at unit costs, personnel costs, material costs, equipment costs, mailing costs, etc. If, for example, an individual is attempting to determine the cost of mailing out new contracts to several hundred vendors with whom the agency deals, the following costs may have to be considered, among others:

- *Duplication costs per duplicated copy.*

- *Salary costs of writing new contract.*

- *Salary costs of typing contracts.*

- *Costs of new contract forms.*

- *Costs of envelopes.*

- *Costs of writing departmental letters.*

Time. Time is usually calculated in terms of the personnel costs or salaries paid. The basic periods of time hours, days, weeks, months, years are quite often combined in terms of man-hours, man-weeks, man-years, etc., to enable the numbers of hour units to be multiplied by salary allocations. Equipment time, particularly in this age of computers, can be quite expensive.

Past Precedent. This is a category relating together data on similar situations in the past, and to consider the decisions arrived at in those situations for their bearing on the decision to be made in the present.

Procedures. These are also important. Most public-service organizations have certain ways of accomplishing functions or providing services. They have been proven over a period of time to be most appropriate to particular situations. Here, too, is where organizational policy making may be involved and possibly changed and modified.

Leadership. This would include the directions and decisions which brought about a particular situation, and permit review of the factors which were present when prior decisions were made.

Quality. The quality of facts is important. There must be an assurance that the right data, and the most applicable figures and information, are available.

Productivity. This category would enable a comparison between various activities which would bring about particular results. It would provide an opportunity to look at the output of a department or project team.

In pulling together like items, one can see trends, certain facts which may be more important than others, and areas where there are gaps in the information.

In organizing facts, the following questions should be asked:

- Which facts are related to each other?

- Are these facts related to any not listed?

- What is the extent of their relationship?

- Are they relevant to this situation?

- What is the level of reliability of the facts?

- Can the problem be more clearly defined with the information listed?

- How can it be done?
- How much time is there for further organization?
- Are these facts recurring or one time events?

D. *Stating the Real Problem*. Having examined the data, the decision-maker is now in a position to state the *real* problem or situation with which he has to deal. He now knows whether he has a problem, or just a misunderstanding. Was the original statement just a symptom, or was it a real situation? It might be that there are several problems. Whatever the situation, it must be stated in clear and simple terms. It should be written down.

A problem is a situation which deviates from an expected standard, or norm of desired performance. In decision making, one starts with an *apparent* problem. The decision maker gathers more information in order to more accurately identify the situation with which he is going to deal.

Is there a real problem? or just symptoms? The data have been gathered and organized. Now it is necessary to zero in on the actual situation, and to see whether there is a real problem. Was the initial identification a symptom of a problem, or was it a real cause? Is there one problem, or several?

If the decision-maker neglected to gather the facts, and then to organize, analyze, and categorize them, he might find himself working on the wrong situation. He could spend a great deal of time and effort on symptoms, and could actually be working on the wrong problem. Certainly, he could overlook a number of relevant factors.

If a medical doctor spent all of his time studying symptoms, he might be too late to address an actual problem and his patient could die. Similarly, in a public-service organization, *if too much time and energy is spent in chasing symptoms instead of causes, problems can become crises.*

What objective is to be achieved? Remember, one must still think about decision making in terms of fulfilling objectives.

When it is known what kind of performance should be achieved, and what kind of performance has been received, the necessary effort is simple merely to measure the difference between those two points. The decision-maker must identify the deviation and its extent. He will also have to specifically state the standard, or *norm,* toward which he is trying to return.

In other words, not only does he have to state the problem to which he is going to address himself, but he must specifically state the objective he wants to achieve.

In the previous illustration of the public-service organization and the communication problems between the accountants and managers, the objectives could, perhaps, be restated in this manner: *it is necessary to design a realistic and accurate budget for costs.*

This stage would complete the problem identification part of the decision-making process. Now, he can get on with decision-making itself.

E. Developing Alternative Solutions. With the *real* problem determined and stated, the decision-maker is now in a position to begin the development of alternative solutions. Notice that there is an "s" on the end of "solution." Decision-makers should be interested in as many solutions to a problem as can be developed.

This particular phase of the decision making process should be very free-wheeling. It should produce a number of ideas. The decision-maker should keep his mind open. He should not be too judgmental, but should avoid premature criticism. *Criticism given too early can destroy new ideas that could be beneficial.*

Picture a staff meeting, where the assistant director of the agency presents an entirely new approach to providing recreational opportunities for senior citizens. He is interrupted by his superior, the director, who tells him that his idea is ridiculous. It is unlikely that he would ever bring up the subject again unless he were extremely persistent and unafraid of the director. *Creative thinking can be squelched by a superior who criticizes without having much of a basis for criticism.*

The number of alternatives that can be developed at any one point in time is a function of how much time is spent in developing these alternatives. It's always helpful to stop and ask: "If I didn't have any rules to follow in this organization, would I handle the situation any differently?" Or, "What else could I do?" Perhaps it is desirable to modify several previously stated alternatives to produce one better alternative.

Present all alternatives for consideration. By considering all ideas as initially feasible, they can be brought out into the open. Such occasions are often called brain storming sessions. Regardless of how silly an idea might seem at first, perhaps when it is considered in the light of other possibilities it may turn out to be a fairly useable solution; or maybe a portion of that idea might be able to be combined with another idea and thereby produce the ultimate solution.

What, for example, would have happened if someone stifled the idea of the paper clip? "Isn't that stupid, who'd want to hold pieces of paper together with bent up wire?" Evidently, people laughed at Columbus, and his idea of a round world; they laughed at John Fulton and his steamship; and even at a young man named Fosbury, who high-jumped backwards. Regardless of ridicule, however, each of these men, in his solution to the problem at hand, succeeded in his particular project.

How many people have been shot-down in creative projects, by comments such as these: "We've tried it and it didn't work," "That's against policy," "It would cost too much," "He hasn't got the experience," "He"'s too young."

List the Alternatives. Looking at the positive side of the argument, there should be positive consideration of all methods, objects, and persons available, to satisfy the needs of decision-making. Once again, write down all of the alternatives, so that they can be comprehensively considered.

To do this, one can list all of the alternatives across the top of a chart and then systematically consider all the factors under each alternative. This chart, or *matrix,* as it is called, can then be used to evaluate the best solution.

As an example, let us assume legislation is passed in each state to award home and business loans and educational benefits to veterans of the Vietnam war. Then a matrix somewhat like this can be made:

	ALTERNATIVES				
	#1	#2	#3	#4	#5
Staff involved					
Labor costs					
Material costs					
Equipment costs					
Services included					
Services excluded					
facilities needed					
Number of veterans processed per day					
Publicity requirements					
Applicable policy					
New policies needed,					
etc.					

The list can be long, but it is well worth it. If, for example, one is considering attending a community college or university, but can't make up his mind. He can develop a chart with all of the things that are important to him on the side of the chart, and the schools under consideration acros the top. Then a five-point scale can *be* applied to each item, with five being the highest mark and zero the lowest. The school with the most points might be the most likely alternative under all the prevailing circumstances. Still, one cannot be completely definite on this basis alone, so it is necessary to move to the next step in the decision-making process, that of selection.

F. Selecting the Best Alternative Solution. The most important part of the decision-making process is the selection of the most appropriate alternative: *deciding.* This is the stage during which criticism is appropriate. Judgment must be made on all facets of the problem and the alternative solutions. The effectiveness of each of the solutions must be evaluated in terms of the objectives towards which the decision-maker is oriented. He must look carefully at, and criticize severely, such items as cost, timeliness, workability, acceptability, and implementation.

- Can the solution be made to work?
- Will the staff cooperate?
- Will those who are served make the necessary adjustments?
- Are there the skills in the organization to carry out the program?

List the Consequences of the Decision. As these and other items are considered, it is desirable to write down all of the consequences of each of the decisions. List the pro's and con's. It is not enough to add them together and make a decision on that basis, such as in the selection of a college, in the previous section. Not only does one use some type of scale, but he assigns different weights to different items. Using the previous college selection chart, the decision-maker might have to weight costs higher than the availability of co-educational dormitories, or the scholastic reputation of the school over the strength of its football team.

Be a Devil's Advocate. The more desirable alternatives should be scrutinized in a negative way. Take the opposite position, that is, play the *devil's advocate.* Mentally implement the plan and consider the adverse consequences.

Take one of the most favorable-looking alternatives. Ask:

- "Will it affect other departments?"
- "What could go wrong?"
- "What are the potential sources of breakdown?"
- "What new problem might it create?"
- "Where would the resistance be?"

Consider the extent to which these consequences will probably come about and the degree of seriousness of each one. Select second and even third choices in order to plan for contingencies.

Scrutinize the Final Alternative Thoroughly . Once the alternatives have been narrowed to only one, which appears to fill the need, then this one alternative should be subjected to one final round of positive questions:

- Will this decision fulfill the original goal?
- Can the agency live with the decision permanently?
- Is the timing of the decision right?
- Does the decision bring about the greatest benefit for the greatest number?

Involve Your Superiors. It is often necessary and desirable to go to the superiors with the decision. Ordinarily, the problem would be presented, with the attendant factors affecting it, and the alternative solutions which could resolve it. Then the decision-maker would indicate his reasons, with their consequences, for selection of the particular alternative.

G. Implement the Decision. After a decision is made, it must be implemented. The necessary steps must be initiated to carry it out. The whole management cycle of planning, organizing, and controlling must be brought into action, as well as other available management tools.

3. SUMMATION

No phase of the management cycle or any other organizational function could be carried out if decisions were not made. Planning, organizing, controlling, as well as motivating, communicating, and setting standards; these all require endless strings of decisions or choices. This is why the final process of decision making is so important.

Good decisions are the result of understanding responsibilities, involving others, knowing the organization, understanding one's own strengths and weaknesses, and being accountable for decisions made.

In understanding the responsibilities involved, one must know where to get information and be cognizant of the extent to which people can take action.

Through involving others, they gain a sense of ownership in the decision, and become more committed. They remove their defense mechanisms.

Knowing an organization requires an awareness of its organizational history and objectives, where the power centers lie, the limits of one's authority, and the way in which work is actually accomplished.

One's understanding of himself and his own shortcomings insures that he will seek out expertise he does not possess himself, and will develop ways to improve his own skills.

The individual should have this motto: *Remember, when you get right down to it, one person may have to decide – YOU!*

STUDENT LEARNING ACTIVITIES

- Prepare a definition of *decision making,*
- Write a brief paper on the decision-making formula.
- Participate in a class discussion about decision making in a selected public-service agency. Try to identify top, middle, and low-level decisions.
- Prepare a definition of the term *problem.*
- Interview a public-service official to identify a problem within his organization. Follow with a class discussion.
- Prepare a brief paper describing three examples of symptoms and their causes.
- Participate in a problem-solving case study.
- Write a brief paper on why facts must be gathered to aid in the decision-making process.
- Identify the kinds of facts and resources you must use to prepare for making decisions about a teacher-assigned topic.
- Participate in a discussion about fact finding.
- Develop with the class, and have at least 20 students complete, a survey questionnaire with open-ended questions on ways in which your school can be improved. Organize responses according to subject and year ranking of importance.
- Participate in a class discussion on the results of the questionnaire survey.
- After the class has decided on one or more ways in which the school can be improved, prepare a report on one of the objectives including:

  statement of an objective,

  facts needed and how obtained,

  categorizing the facts.
- Deliver an oral version of your report. Respond to questions and comments from the class,
- Choose five articles from the newspaper on five different topics: sports, politics, crime, etc. State the actual problem being addressed.

- Participate in a class discussion about problem identification, and problem statements. Sharpen your problem statements if necessary.

- Participate in a class discussion about problems identified and possible alternative solutions.

- Using the example of the State legislature passing a bill awarding home and business loans and educational benefits to veterans of the Gulf War, develop a set of alternative plans as to how the legislation may be carried out.

TEACHER MANAGEMENT ACTIVITIES

- Have students define *decision making.*

- Assign students a paper on the decision-making formula.

- Conduct a class discussion about decision-making in a selected public service agency.

- Have students prepare their own definitions of the term *problem.*

- Assign students interviews with public-service officials to identify selected organizational problems.

- Conduct a class discussion on problems in public-service organizations.

- Have students develop and discuss reports and three examples of symptoms and their causes.

- Select and assign a case study to the class in problem solving.

- Assign a paper on why facts must be gathered to aid in the decision-making process.

- Prepare a list of considerations in several public-service agencies. Have each student select one consideration around which he will gather essential facts to make a decision.

- Conduct a discussion on fact finding.

- Assign the class a survey project, entitled "How Can Our School be Improved?" Have students develop their own questionnaire and administer it to at least 20 students. Ask them to organize their results according to subject and rank of importance.

- Organize a class discussion on the results of the surveys.

- Once one or more items of possible school improvement have been agreed upon, assign the students a report to contain the following:

statement of an objective,

facts needed and how obtained,

categorizing of facts.

- Organize oral presentations of student reports.
- Assign students the reading of five articles from a newspaper on five different topics: sports, polttfcs, crime, etc. Have them state the actual problem being discussed.
- Conduct a class discussion on problem identification and problem statements.
- Assign a brief paper on the symptoms of five problems and the causes in a public service agency selected by each student.
- Conduct a class discussion on the problems and solutions identified.
- Using the example of the new bill for veterans of the Gulf War, have students develop a set of alternatives.
- Insure that the students are open to new and abstract suggestions.
- Direct oral presentations of students in which they review their original problems, the sources and categories of facts, the alternatives available for solution, their respective consequences, and their ultimate decisions. Have students challenge one another's decisions.

Evaluation Questions
Techniques of Decision Making

Read the problem carefully, and answer each of the following questions.

You are a library assistant. Mrs. Smith, the librarian, has two high school aides, Susan and Mary. Mrs. Smith has told you that she may fire Susan if her attitude does not improve. She complained about Susan's laziness and stated that Susan's work was never finished. Mrs. Smith asked you to talk to Susan about improving her attitude. When you tried to talk to Susan about this, she got upset and went home.

After observing the aides' workload for a few days, you notice that Susan has much more work than Mary.

1. What is the problem? ______________________________
____
____
____

2. Name one solution. ______________________________
____
____
____

3. What are the consequences of this solution? ______________________________
____
____
____

4. List another solution. ______________________________
____
____
____

5. What are the consequences of this solution? ______________________________
____
____
____

6. Which do you think is the best solution? ______________________________
____
____
____

Read the problem carefully, and answer each of the following questions.

You are in charge of the recreation program at the community center. Your job is to keep activities running smoothly. On the daily schedule, one-half hour has been set aside for basketball. While you have stepped out for a moment, ten of the Green Hornets and ten of the Purple Dragons arrived to play basketball. As each group has two teams set up, neither group would give in. Unfortunately, a fight began. The fight ended just as you returned. Each group plans to play tomorrow. You must make a decision.

1. What is the problem? ____________________
2. Name one solution. ____________________
3. What are the consequences of this solution? ____________________
4. List another solution. ____________________
5. What are the consequences of this solution? ____________________
6. Which do you think is the best solution? ____________________

Answer Key

Answers will vary on this test. The instructor may wish to have a discussion after the test, with students justifying their selections. Students may be evaluated on the soundness of their judgement.

BASIC FUNDAMENTALS OF INTERPERSONAL RELATIONSHIPS

TABLE OF CONTENTS

BASIC FUNDAMENTALS OF INTERPERSONAL RELATIONSHIPS

INSTRUCTIONAL OBJECTIVES

1. Ability to distinguish between formal and informal behavior.
2. Ability to identify the important factors in communicating with people.
3. Ability to understand how defense mechanisms affect communication with others.
4. Ability to identify the roles played in effective person-to-person communication.
5. Ability to acquire the human relations skills needed for getting along with others both on and off the job.
6. Ability to establish greater personal effectiveness with others so as to develop better cooperation and superior-subordinate relationships in public-service working situations.
7. Ability to recognize the mutual dependence of individuals on each other.
8. Ability to form positive attitudes toward the worth and dignity of every human being.
9. Ability to become aware of how feelings affect one's own behavior, as well as one's relationships with other people.
10. Ability to use an understanding of human relationships to effectively work with people.
11. Ability to improve communications with others by developing greater effectiveness in dealing with people in the world of public service.

CONTENT

INTRODUCTION

Perhaps the single most important skill that a public-service worker, or anyone for that matter, needs, is the ability to get along with other people. "Person-to-person" relationships are the building blocks of all social interactions between two-individuals. If there is one essential ingredient for success in life, both on and off the job, it is developing greater effectiveness in dealing with people.

The skill of the teacher is critical to the success of this unit. He should establish a permissive and non-threatening group climate in which free communication and behavior can take place. The importance of this unit cannot be over stated. The overall objective is to establish greater personal effectiveness with others and to develop better co-operative and superior-subordinate relationships in the public-service occupations. Obtaining greater "self-awareness" is a large part of this goal. Because interpersonal relations are affected by a variety of factors, some attention should be given initially to basic rules of conduct and behavior on the job.

1. INTERPERSONAL CONDUCT AND BEHAVIOR ON THE JOB

Most public-service agencies have clearly defined rules and regulations. The behavior of the public-service worker is often guided by the established procedures and directives of that individual agency. In many cases, even individual departments or units will have procedures manuals, which regulate conduct and office work.

Formal Organization of the Office

At one point or another, most public-service employees either work directly in an office, or come in frequent contact with other people working in an administrative or staff office. Students should become familiar with the organizational structure of the occupational groups in which they are planning on working. A park worker, for example, must know about the organization of the Parks Department–what kinds of staff or administrative services are provided, what about training, what are the safety rules, what goes into personnel records, etc. Preparing a flow chart of the relationships between different positions in a particular agency is one way of learning about the organization of that office or agency.

Office as a Setting for formal and Informal Relations

It is necessary to become aware of the different kinds of social relations shared with co-workers and the public. Some co-workers, for example, are seen only at work, and others are seen socially after work and/or on weekends. Factors that determine which co-workers become *personal* friends and which are just *work* friends should be considered and discussed.

On the other hand, a public-service worker usually has more formal relationships with the public with whom he comes into contact. Consider the relationships of the preschool teacher's aide and his students, the library helper and his library patrons, the police cadet and the general public, etc. In each of these cases, the public expects the public-service worker to help them with a particular service.

Although the distinction between formal and informal social relationships is not always clear, one should be sensitive to the fact that both kinds of relationships affect the behavior of the public and the public-service employee, Normally, the very organization of the public-service office helps to create a social climate for developing working relationships of a formal nature, and personal relationships with co-workers and the public which are of a more impersonal nature.

Office Behavior

Specific kinds of behavior relate to these formal and informal relationships with other people. Typically, the formal relationship is well prescribed and regulated by procedures or directives. The license interviewer, as an example, has specific questions to ask, and specific information to obtain from the applicant. Their relationship can be described as formal or prescribed by regulation. On the other hand, other office behavior can best be described as informal and non-prescribed (or *free*). Interpersonal relations in this case are often more personal and relaxed by their very nature.

2. INTERPERSONAL COMMUNICATION - THE MEANING

Interpersonal communication can be defined as a two-way flow of information from person-to-person. One cannot Study human relations without examining the constant relationships that man has with other people; the individual does not exist in a vacuum. Most of man's psychological and social needs are met through dealings with other people. In fact, one psychiatrist (Harry Stark Sullivan) has developed a theory of personality based upon interpersonal situations. This viewpoint, known as the *Interpersonal Theory of Psychiatry,* claims that personality is essentially the enduring pattern of continued interpersonal relationships between people. This interpersonal behavior is all that can be observed as personality.

Importance of Face-to-Face Contacts

The very phrase. *Public Service Occupations,* suggests frequent face-to-face contacts with not only the general public, but with co-workers as well. With possibly a few exceptions, practically every public-service employee encounters frequent person-to-person contacts both on and off the job. The ability to get along with people is a very important part of public-service work.

Listening Techniques

Effective listening is a critical part of interpersonal communications. Listening is an active process, requiring not only that one must *pay attention* to what is being said, but that one must also *listen* for the meaning of what is being said. Almost one-half of the total time spent communicating, (reading, writing, speaking, or listening) is spent in listening.

Even though people get considerable practice at listening, they don't do too well at it. Many studies have shown that, on the average, a person retains only about 25 percent of a given speech after only 10 minutes have elapsed. Most people forget three quarters of what they hear in a relatively short period of time. Clearly, people need to improve their listening skills if they are to become more effective in their relations with other people.

3. FACTORS IN INTERPERSONAL COMMUNICATION

There are a number of components that affect the person-to-person relationship. Some of the factors common to both the sender and the receiver in a person-to-person communication are:

The Attitudes and Emotions of the Individuals

For example - two people are shouting and screaming at each other - how effective is their interpersonal communication?

- *The Needs and Wants of the People Communicating*

Both the sender and receiver have unique desires, some open, and some hidden from the other person. These needs can and do strongly influence interpersonal relationships.

- *The Implied Demands of the Sender and Receiver*

  An important factor in interpersonal communications involves requests or demands. How are these demands handled? What are some typical responses to demands? These factors are common to both the sender and the receiver in interpersonal relations and affect the individual behavior of the people communicating.

The Choice of Words of the Conversant

One's choice of words can have a direct bearing on the interpersonal communication. The vocabulary one uses in interpersonal relationships should be appropriate for the occasion. For example, a preschool teacher's aide would not use the same vocabulary in talking to a three-year-old, as she would in talking to the preschool teacher.

How Each Sees the Other

The process of communicating from person-to-person is greatly influenced by the perception that the sender and receiver have of each other. The feelings that a person has toward the other person are reflected in his tone of voice, choice of words, and even in his *body language.* A reference book mentioned in the resource section of this unit, *How to Read a Person Like a Book,* deals with the importance of body language in person-to-person relationships.

The Right Time and Place

Another factor that may be important in interpersonal relationships is the timing of the communication. For example, one of the first things a supervisor should do if he wants to talk over a problem with his subordinate, is ask the question: "Is this the right time and place?" Problems should not generally be discussed in the middle of an office, where other employees, or the public, can hear the discussion. Personal problems should be discussed only in private.

The Effect of Past Experience

In general, the quality of the person-to-person transaction will depend upon the past experience of the individuals. Human beings have acquired most of their opinions, assumptions, and value judgments through their relationships with other people. Past experience not only helps to teach people about effective interpersonal relationships, it is also often responsible for the irrational prejadices that a person displays. A strong bias usually blocks the interpersonal relationship if the subject of the communication concerns that particular bias.

The Effect of Personal Differences

An additional factor in interpersonal communications involves the intelligence and other personal differences of the people communicating. An example of such a personal difference is the *objectivity* of the people involved, as compared with their *subjectivity.* One person may try to be very fair and objective in discussing a point with another person, yet this other person is, at the same time, taking everything personally and being very subjective in his viewpoint. It is almost as if an adult was talking to an angry child.

Such differences can impede the communications flow between two people. In fact, all the factors mentioned in communications should be examined as to whether they block or facilitate interpersonal relationships. *The most effective interpersonal relationships are those that are adult-like in their character.*

4. DEFENSE MECHANISMS IN INTERPERSONAL RELATIONS

Defense mechanisms are attempts to defend the individual from anxiety. They are essentially a reaction to frustration - a self-deception.

Causes for Defense Mechanisms

In order to help understand some of the causes for defense mechanisms, remember the basic human needs:

- *Biological or physiological needs* - hunger, water, rest, etc.
- *Psychological or social needs* - status, security, affection, justice etc.

Fear of failure in any of these basic needs appears to be related to the development of defense mechanisms; attitudes toward failure, in turn, originate out of the fabric of childhood experience. The social and cultural conditions encountered during childhood determine the rewards and controls which fill one's later life. These childhood experiences, and their resultant consequences, affect personality development, the individual's value system, and his definition of acceptable goals.

Individuals who are dominated by the fear of failure may react by using one of these defense mechanisms:

- *Rationalization* - making an impulsive action seem logical.

- *Projection* - assigning one's traits to others.

- *Identification* - assuming someone else's favorite qualities are their own.

Results of Use of Defense Mechanisms

A common factor to all defense mechanisms is their quality of *self-deception.* People cling to their impulses and actions, perhaps disguising them so that they become socially acceptable. Their defense mechanisms can be found in the everyday behavior of most normal people and, of course, have *direct influences* on interpersonal relationships.

A person, for example, who is responsible for a particular job makes a mistake, and the work doesn't get done. When confronted with the problem by his supervisor, the individual puts the blame on someone or something else. This is a very common form of a defense mechanism.

Defense mechanisms can sometimes have *negative influences* on interpersonal communications. They can contribute to the individual forming erroneous opinions about the other person's motives. These mechanisms can alter the perceptions and evaluations made about the individual by other people, Ways to understand these mechanisms must be sought; one solution is to become more aware of the common defense mechanisms, and to become less defensive through greater acceptance of others.

5. THE INFLUENCES OF ROLE-PLAYING IN INTERPERSONAL RELATIONS

Everyone wears a mask and plays a certain role or roles in life. Even if the role one plays is to be himself, that particular form of behavior can still be considered a role. As a public-service employee, one's role is to serve the public. This can be done in a number of ways. Some of the factors involved in public-service roles will be mentioned below:

Exploring Superior-Subordinate Relations

Public-service employees are accountable for their actions. From the entry-level public administrative analysis trainee, to the President of the United States, every public servant must be accountable to either an immediate supervisor, a governing body, or to the public itself. Entry-level public-service employees gain experience and get promoted, but they continue to be subordinates and responsible for their actions, even though they also become supervisors and have people working for them.

Simulation exercises can be developed which will examine the perceptions of the superior by the subordinate. *Authority* and *power* factors may enter in here, as the superior also perceives the subordinate in a particular way. *Dominance* and *need* factors are at work in superior-subordinate relationships, and the style of leadership used *(autocratic, democratic,* or *lassiez-faire)* is a form of leadership role.

Peer relationships can be explored through simulation exercises. The ways in which co-workers perceive each other and the resultant effect on cooperation is one area to be examined. Ways to establish a climate or environment for effective, cooperative relations should be sought.

It is desirable also to simulate, for better comprehension, interpersonal communications with the general public. Role-playing techniques, which permit the exploration of person-to-person relationships, are highlighted in the following section on simulation exercises.

Interpersonal Relations Achieved Through Simulation

The preparation of students for entry-level public-service occupations must include an opportunity to experience meaningful interpersonal relations. Public-service employees, whether office or field workers, experience personal relationships with other people every day. The initial success of the public-service worker will depend in large measure upon his ability to interact effectively with others in the office or field. Accordingly, a principle objective of simulation exercises for entry-level public-service education is to have the student acquire the necessary interpersonal relations skills that make for success in all public-service occupations.

When developing a model public-service simulation with the principal objective being to improve favorable interpersonal relations, certain criteria must be established. These criteria may be stated as follows:

- *Interpersonal relations must be the principal component of the simulation*. Provision must be made for students to interact with others in an office interpersonal setting so that they may work and communicate effectively with one another.

- *The simulation must be as realistic as possible*. Realism can best be accomplished by simulating an actual public-service operation in as many areas as possible.

- *Originality must play an important part*. Model simulations, currently in use, must not be copied in an effort to maintain simplicity.

- *The simulation must be interesting*. Students must be motivated to participate in the simulation and to be enthusiastic about its operation.

- *The simulation must be unstructured*. Provision must be made to allow for an awareness of events as they take place. Students must learn to cope with a situation without prior knowledge that the situation will occur.

In order for the teacher to determine if the model public-service simulation developed has, in fact, improved interpersonal relations, the simulation must be evaluated in terms of meeting the established objectives.

6. MEASURING INTERPERSONAL RELATIONS

Survey of Interpersonal Values

A valid and reliable instrument for measuring interpersonal relations, such as the *Survey of Interpersonal Values,* may be used for this purpose. This instrument is intended for grades 9-12, and is designed to measure the relative importance of the major factored interpersonal value dimensions. These values include both the subject's relations with others and others with himself. The value dimensions considered are:

- *Support*--being treated with understanding, encouragement, kindness, and consideration.

- *Conformity*--doing what is socially correct, accepted, and proper.

- _Recognition_--being admired, looked up to, considered important, and attracting favorable notice.

- _Independence_--being able to do what one wants to do, making one's own decisions, doing things in one's own way.

- _Benevolence_--doing things for other people, sharing, and helping.

- _Leadership_--being in charge of others, having authority or power.

A pretest on interpersonal values is administered before the model public-service simulation actually begins, and the same test is administerd as a post-test after a stipulated period of time. By comparison of results, and through the use of applicable statistics, the gain in behavior modification in interpersonal relations can be determined, as a result of using the model public-service simulation.

Analysis of Interpersonal Behavior

Public-service employees should be aware of their own needs, and of the needs of other people. They should be able to recognize situations or behavior calling for professional help, and be able to refer people to such appropriate help. New employees must be able to use their knowledge of person-to-person relationships to effectively work with people.

In order to become more effective in interpersonal relationships, students must gain an understanding of:

- _Self-evaluation_ - to be able to assess their own strengths and weaknesses.

- _Group Evaluation_ - as a class to be able to evaluate other individuals' competencies in interpersonal communications.

- _Correction of own self-perception_ - to be able to do something about the knowledge and attitudes formed by adjusting their individual behavior.

STUDENT LEARNING ACTIVITIES

- Define formal and informal social behavior.
- List the important factors in interpersonal communication.
- View and discuss the film strip, *Your Educational Goals, No. 2: Human Relationships.*
- Role play in alternate supervisor-subordinate relationships practicing effective interpersonal communication.
- Write an essay on "Defense mechanisms affect interpersonal relationships."
- View the film, *The Unanswered Question,* and discuss human relationships afterwards.
- Listen to a discussion of structured interpersonal communications and evaluate the effectiveness of the person-to-person relationship.

- In small groups, discuss the ways in which people are mutually dependent on each other,
- Use simulation exercises to practice interpersonal relations.
- List the different kinds of roles and games played in interpersonal communications.
- Debate the statement: *Understanding person-to-person relations is one of the most important skills a person can acquire for success in life.*
- Discuss how understanding interpersonal relationships can help a person to effectively work with people.
- Define the role of recognizing one's own feelings in relation to others.

TEACHER MANAGEMENT ACTIVITIES

- Have the students define formal and informal social behavior.
- Show transparencies on interpersonal relations, *(Social Sensitivity lour Relationship with Others)* and discuss concepts afterwards.
- Assign written exercises on the important factors in interpersonal communication.
- Set up role-playing exercises on subordinate-supervisor roles in effective interpersonal communication.
- Encourage small-group discussions of the ways people are mutually dependent on each other.
- Show a movie on human relationships *(The Unanswered Question)* and discuss key points afterwards.
- Separate the class into teams to debate such statements as: Understanding interpersonal relations is one of the most important skills a person can acquire for success in life.
- Encourage individual study and reading in interpersonal relationships.
- Assign an essay on the worth and dignity of man in interpersonal relations.
- Bring in public-service workers who deal with others to talk to the class about the value of effective interpersonal communications.

10

Evaluation Questions

Fill in the crossword puzzle below.

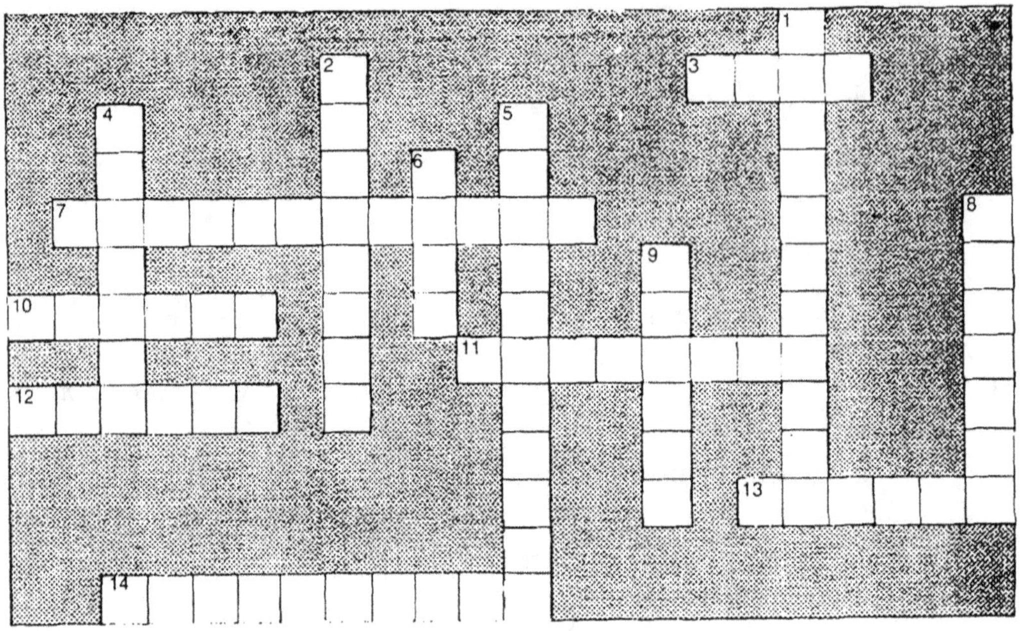

ACROSS:

3. A strong prejudice or ______ can block good relationships.
7. Being abie to do what one wants to do satisfies the need tor ______.
10. One's _______ of words should be correct for the occasion.
11. Friends usually have an ______ relationship.
12. In talking over problems with others, is important.
13. Everyone needs to feel ______.
14. ______ is assigning one's traits to others.

DOWN:

1. We ______ when we try to make our actions seem logical.
2. When we assume someone's qualities as our own we ______ with that person.
4. Individuals ______ when they do what is socially proper.
5. When we attract favorable attention, we gain ______
6. Some people have a strong ______ of failure.
8. ______ mechanics help to protect a person from anxiety.
9. A public service worker usually has a ______ relationship with the public.

Answer Key

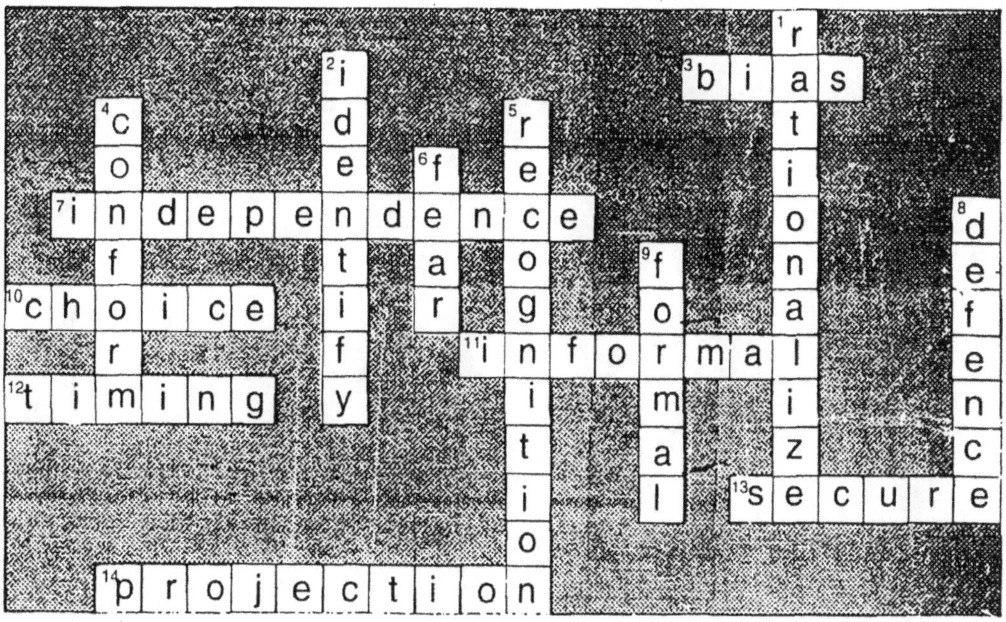
1 rationalize
2 identify
3 bias
4 conform
5 recognition
6 fear
7 independence
8 defence
9 formal
10 choice
11 informal
12 timing
13 secure
14 projection

www.ingramcontent.com/pod-product-compliance
Lightning Source LLC
Chambersburg PA
CBHW082039300426
44117CB00015B/2537
* 9 7 8 1 7 9 9 3 6 6 2 6 3 *